Mystic Saints of India : 9

Tulsidas

B K Chaturvedi

Series Editor : (Dr.) Mahendra

Books For All

Delhi-110052

Distributed by
D. K. Publishers Distributors Pvt. Ltd.
24, Ansari Road, Darya Ganj,
New Delhi-110 002
Phs. : 327 8368, 326 1465, 327 8584
Fax : 326 4368
E-mail : dkpd@del3.vsnl.net.in
Web site:www.dkpd.com.

First Published : 2002

ISBN 81-7386-250-8(Tulsidas)
ISBN 81-7386-231-1 (Series)

Published by :
Books For All
(an imprint of Low Price Publications)
A-6, Nimri Commercial Centre,
Near Ashok Vihar Phase-IV, Delhi-110 052
Ph. : 740 1672, 745 2453
E-mail : lpp@nde.vsnl.net.in
Web site:www.lppindia.com.

Printed at
D. K. Fine Art Press Pvt. Ltd.
Delhi-110052 Ph. 745 2451

Printed in India

Preface

Tulsidas is believed to be the crown-jewel Saint Poet of entire Hindi Literature and his 'Sriram charita manas' is accorded the status of a divine book by the Hindus. Of course, he is one of those poets whose creations command global respect but the present book is a humble attempt to reveal all aspects of his personality, apart from the representative selection of his creations. Since, he has written quite copiously and only in lyrical form, it was a difficult task to select his poems, prayers etc. in such a way as to reveal the complete span of his creative scale. The criterion of the selection of the poems has mainly been their popularity. The translation of the text has been done keeping in mind the sensibility and the basic background of our Hindi and English readership. Since, he has influenced the rustic and the scholar alike, in order to make his impact realised by the readership one of his folk-bhajans has also been selected, although its authenticity - being a Tulsidas creation - is suspect. Nevertheless, the content and style bear an unmistakable stamp of Tulsidas.

It is hoped that our discerning readership will also accord this book the same warm response as it has accorded the other books of this series; Mystic Saints of India. Lastly, the author/translator conveys his deep gratitude to Pradeep Mittal of Books For All for allowing him total freedom and their help.

B K Chaturvedi

SERIES' EDITOR'S NOTE

In 1963, Dr. Radhakrishnan, the President of India, declared in Bombay, "The time has come for all countries to work towards making the world a single home for Humanity.....Economics, Politics and transport have done their jobs. But we have to do as to give a soul to the world which has found a body, you can give it if you are truly Indian." We Indians are proud to have so many mystic saints who contributed to the upliftment of humanity.

In Indian thought, there are two modes in which we acquire knowledge: Argument and Experiment. Both these modes, together with experience play an important role in the development of mankind. Saints of India, through their arguments, tried to communicate their experiences to human beings. This represents an adventure in thinking.

This series, it is hoped, will enable the reader, eastern or western, to understand and appreciate currents of Indian thought by depicting the life and writings of different saints. We have tried to portray the true picture of Indian culture. I am really thankful to all those who have helped in preparing and publishing these books, as they will not only propagate the ideas of Indian saints, but also help in making mankind a better race.

Our world becomes wider, our imagination richer and our life more colourful and more zestful as a result of our companionship with these saints, who are the travellers of the spirit and the pioneers of thought.

25.7.01 **(DR.) MAHENDRA**

Content

1

Tulsidas: A Par Excellence Poet With Universal Vision

Tulsidas was not merely a class poet but one of those 'Atlases' of the Hindu society who prevented it from collapsing when all the social, religious and moral norms were going to dogs in the trauma of the consolidation of an-till then- alien rule. It was his magnum opus: 'SRI RAMCHARITA MANAS' which gave the Hindu community a hope to live under the most trying circumstances. Had it not been for Tulsidas, said Gandhiji, the entire Hindu society would have disintegrated and perished out of immense frustration and a deep anguish of purposelessness.

As a matter of fact, his age was marked by division and hence frustration reigned at all levels. The Hindu society was divided with their diehard religious leanings and beliefs, the social norms had become sullied with many erroneous dogmas and politically the whole country appeared despondent with the consolidation of the Mughal rule. There was no central authority to set right the disorder. The kings, believed to be totally submissive to their alien overlords, could not be the object of adoration by the people and the religious heads of different faiths had the mutual cut-throat competition overwhelming them. There used to be open battles between the followers of 'Rama Cult' and the believer of Shankar's supremacy in the Hindu pantheism. The sacred books were being interpreted to accord greater honour to the chosen deity of one sect. A kind of enervating ennui had set in all walks of life. The people were thoroughly confused with no source available to dispel their misapprehensions. The ruling kings had lost their awe and veneration and the religious heads their credibility and appeal due to their parochial vision. Socially the situation was getting anarchic and confused. Although the Muslim population had begun to intermingle with the native population their convictions were yet to emerge out of the melting pot. It was during this time that inborn xenophobia had also begun to show its effect in alarming proportions and with the political authority beginning to pass into the hands of the invaders, the social tensions became all the more pronounced. Each section and sub-section of different faiths had started to denounce the other as inferior with unconcealed contempt. This disintegrating process not only created schism in the main faith of the land, the Hinduism, but also crevices began to appear in the various sub divisions and communities that developed within one fold of a faith. Among the Hindus the subsections: Shaakta, Shaiva and Vaishnavas had taken cudgels against each other.

In fact this was the period when despite appearing politically stable with the advent of Emperor Akbar on the throne of Delhi, the whole country was highly destabilised internally. Even Akbar had sensed this brewing danger. In order to create a sort of order in religion he also started his all-unifying faith called 'Din-i-Ilahi'. Nevertheless, the masses began to be severely inflicted with mutual rivalry among the various centres of faith working with self-proclaimed authority. There was no unified code for social norm. Jungle law was prevailing all around and the common masses were feeling insecure at all levels. History bears testimony to the fact that when the people - particularly of the orient - feel disenchanted with secular authority they invariably look heavenward for relief. Hence, the onset of the Bhakti movement whose central theme was total dependence on the Almighty. The people found no escape from the suffocating decay of the values and so they began to indulge in deeper prayers to the divine authority to set the chaos in order. This, naturally, led to the growth of various poets, thinker-philosopher seeking recourse in pure devotion to awaken the hidden virtues in man.

Tulsidas was, perhaps, the giant among them. While he was not an iconoclast like Kabir was, he, nevertheless, sought to make man truer to himself by deriding all kinds of pretensions and hypocrisy. Like Soordas he believed in the worship of a God with form but unlike Soordas or Meera, he was equally concerned with the depravity setting in society and tried through his poems to remove all the same. Moreover, he was a visionary and had realised that the basic cause of social disharmony lay enshrined in the parochial interpretation to suit the interpreters' vested interest. He was convinced that the Pundits and other religious heads, in their extreme selfishness, had made the sacred texts their exclusive preserve which they interpreted in such a way as suited them most. Since most of the sacred texts of the Hindus were in Sanskrit, a language which the common people couldn't follow, he decided to bring out the essence of all the Puranas, Upanishads, Gita, Mahabharata and Ramayana in the language commonly understood by the people. It was, indeed, a momentous task never even attempted earlier by anyone. The sacred lore or the Sanatana Dharama - as Hinduism should be called, since it seeks to ensure 'perenniality' of this unique faith delineating ideal for all species and norms for every society - is encompassed in very huge tomes. There are 18 Puranas, many Upanishadas, 4 Vedas, Gita, Ramayana and Mahabharata. Vetting all these books to cater to the need of the times and rendering their essence in a language, at once gripping and easily understandable, needed a full institution of the choicest brains. But Tulsidas did it all alone, unaided by anyone. On the contrary, he was frequently disturbed by the unsocial elements at the behest of those selfish pundits who felt their source of convenient wherewithal seriously threatened with the sacred text made understandable by all. Yet, undaunted by all such disturbances and - as it is believed, helped in his mission by Lord Hanuman, he kept on creating tomes of verses to make the common man capable to sift reality from the shadow and grain from the chaff. He is credited with having written more than a dozen books of verses. His popular creations are: *Sriramcharita manas*, *Vinaya Patrika*, *Kavitavali*, *Dohavali*, *Hanuman Bahuka*, *Ramlala Nahachhoo, Hanuman Chalisa* but the most popular among them is, and shall ever remain, *Sriramcharita manas*, called his *'magnum opus.'* It contains not only the Rama-Katha which forms its basic structure but all that is perceivable in the Hindu sacred texts and lore. His poetry-books, particularly 'Sriramcharita manas' is the most widely acclaimed and universally accepted work of India's most popular language - Hindi. It is an epic of universal and irresistable appeal, virtually the Bible for nearly half a billion people. It represents the quintessence of Hindu social culture at its congenial best; it is a deeply moving sociological delineation of Hindu ethos and psyche at its aesthetic acme. What is the specialty of Tulsi's creations is their capacity to overwhelm the illiterate and the learned alike. They are admired by the vast majority of the Hindus, nay, the entire Indian community. Particularly *Sriramcharita manas* represents the sole norm of conduct; inextricably interwoven into life's character and speech of the vast multitudes for over a period of half a millennium. It propagates a simple and sublime religion and, according to, Grierson, the most renowned critic of Medieval Hindi literature, its most remarkable achievement, in the age of perverse morality, was its stern morality in every walk of life.

Tulsidas encompassed into his literature not only the polished gems of ancient thought but also the common-place graffitti of his times. It is because of this smoothness that many of his lines have become the idioms and oft-quoted phrases for all times. For example, see 'Ka barakha jab krisi sukhane' [What is the use of the rains when the crop has already withered] or 'Kouoo nripa hoya hamen ka hanee' [How does it adversely affect us who is eventually enthroned as the king]. These phrases resound the Indian Parliament and the village chaupals alike. It is the sheer range and magnitude of Tulsidas's literature that is so amazing. Can one man write all these plain-truths of life with such arresting simplicity that goes direct to heart? His infinite quotability is unmatched even by Ghalib. Tulsidas has an apt saying for every occasion, situation and circumstance. With such a command he chooses his words to convey the feeling that at times it is irrenderable in any other language.

Tulsidas's style added another feather to his cap from the side of the captivated critics. Of course, most of his thoughts are taken from other works in Sanskrit but his style makes his used phrases more effective than even the original. Given below are some examples in which Tulsidas has deftly translated Sanskrit text into the *lingua franca* of his times.

The Gita:

Yada yada hi dharmasya
Glaanir bhavati Bharatah |
Abhyuthaanamdharmasya
Tadaat maanam srijamyaham ||
Paritranaya sadhoonam |
Vinaashaaye cha duskritaam
Dharmasansthapanarthaya
Sambhavami yuge yuge ||

See this famous saying of the Gita rendered in a simple language by Tulsidas in his 'Sriramcharita manas'.

Jab-jab hoi dharam kee hanee
Badhahin asur adham abhimanee
Tab-tab Hari dhari vividha shareera
Harehin Kripanidhi sajjan-peera |

How faithfully rendered it is with the additional advantage of folk-music thrown in the lines!

Now consider the following lines from the Bhavishya Purana

The Bhavishya Purana:
Mookam karoti vaachalem
Pangu langhayate girim |
Yat-kripa tamahan vande
Paramanandan Madhavam |

Tulsi renders it the following way in his 'Manas'

Mooka hoyin vachaal
pangu chadahin girivar gahana |
Jasu kripa su dayal
dravahu sakal kali mala dahana ||

Not only these but even the small pithy sayings have been lifted from Sanskrit words and rendered into local language with a telling impact.

The *Brahma Vaivarta Purana* says:

"Brahmananatu hridayam komalam navaneete vata". And Tulsidas with greater emphasis on the noble quality releases the saying from the pro-brahmanic assertion to a more universal one. He writes simply: "Santa hridaya navaneeta samane". He has cleverly replaced 'Brahmana' with Sant (holymen, noble) to make it more universal in appeal and has altogether removed the term 'komala' from his translation simply because butter is even otherwise soft (komal) and use of this adjective was only autological.

In fact there are thousands of such examples which assert that Tulsidas has very rarely been original. Of course, in poetic considerations his style makes Soordas a superior poet than Tulsidas since the former is renowned for his unmatched original and unique similes and metaphors. But if one considers the comparison in the larger terms, Tulsidas still stands head and shoulders above his coeval poets or even the subsequent ones.

Tulsidas appears to simplify the sacred ideas as mentioned in Sanskrit with greater finness. Being well-versed in Sanskrit as also in the local dialects of Hindi: Avadhee, Bhojpuri and Braja-bhasha, etc., his vocabulary appears truly astounding. On top of it he would fit the words so beautifully in his lines as to make them musically also very apt. Using a three to four page long running, continued metaphors in the unrefined local dialects with an enhanced impact needed a genius which he was.

He also did not mind borrowing phrases from other languages or thoughts as were prevalent during his time. His emphasis on non-violence appears to have been taken from the tenets of Jainism. Kindness to one's neighbour and consideration to all beings are some of the concepts which have been emphasised by Tulsidas as other Indian poets have also done since these concepts were basically imported and were suitably modified. They did figure in the sacred texts of India but not with that emphasis.

Apart from all this, the most significant contribution of Tulsidas had been his ability to remove the differences among the various sects of the Hindu fold which were seemingly threatening the collapse of the society through an internecine struggle. The two most powerful cults of the Hindu faith: 'Shaivism' and 'Vaishnavism' were baying for each other's blood. Kashi used to witness blood riots between the 'Shaivas' and the 'Vaishnavas'. Egged on by the local priests while the Shaivites called Lord Shiv superior to any other deity of the Hindu pantheism, the Vaishnavas hailed Lord Vishnu as the Super God. Tulsidas was sad to see the devotees of different gods clashing. So in order to bring honour to both the deities in all the devotees, whether they be of Lord Shiv or Lord Rama, he repeatedly used the mythological instances to show Lord Ram (the incarnation of Lord Vishnu) worshipping Lord Shiv and Lord Shiv bowing to Lord Vishnu. Time and again he made Lord Ram proclaim:

"Shiv-drohi mam das kahava |
So nar sapanehu mohi na bhava ||

[I can't tolerate the sight of that person even in dreams who calls himself my devotee while showing hostility to Shiv]

Apart from trying to take out these evil trends permeating the society then, he also projected before the people the ideal of every relationship. In this sphere, Tulsidas even scores over Kabir as a social reformer because while Kabir only breaks the images without showing even the semblance of what they ought to be, Tulsidas offers before the people the ideals incarnated in men and women. His Ram is ideal in all respects. Ram in the 'Manas' is not the carbon copy of Valmiki's Ram but surely a brighter version. While Valmiki's Ram may describe his most intimate terms with Sita to make Hanuman—the potential messenger to Sita—realise the depth of his love, not Tulsi's Ram who ever remains a sober and controlled person. Not only Ram but most of the characters as depicted by Tulsidas in his 'Manas' are either noble or getting out of their mean mentality. Whether it was Kaikayee or Manthara, eventually they never appear as villainous or as vamps in the 'Manas'. As a matter of fact, Tulsi's Ram is the most perfect image of man, unsurpassed by any other such heroic image available in the literature of the rest of the world. No wonder even for our Bapu the perfect state was 'Ram-Rajya'. Tulsidas's poems and the epic have always been gaining in popularity and never for a moment appear obsolete in any age even after nearly half a millennium of their creation. The presidents and the peasants, the rulers and ryots all quote Tulsi to assert their point. It is difficult to find any such poet whose range of appeal is so broad and extensive.

Tulsidas stands out as a man of comprehensive and composite vision who tried to resolve the contradictory ideas of his age; who rose above parochial dogmas and sectarian views to bring about a harmony amongst fanatic adherents of religious bigotry through an essentially human approach.

However, sadly enough, despite being such a great poet, reformer, thinker and a visionary and also very popular, no authentic version of his life-story is available even till now. There is much dispute about his place of birth and even about the date of his death. Nevertheless, going by popular legend, available records and the hints about his life-story thrown in his works, his life-story has been 'evoked' which is given in the coming pages.

2

Birth And Early Life Upto Marriage

Near Prayag (modern Allahabad), in the district of Banda, there was a small village called Rajapur. There lived a brahman named Atma Ram Dubey. His wife's name was Hulsi.

It was the Sawan month of the year Samvat 1554 (equivalent to 1498 AD). Atma Ram was a worried person. After much prayer and worship, at last his wife Hulsi became pregnant. He had no son and this truly was a happy news. But he was surprised when she continued to be pregnant even beyond nine months. Dubey Ji hurriedly consulted the local physician and the expert maids to learn that the embryo was still growing even after the stipulated period of normal pregnancy. This further added to Dubeji's worry. He consulted many seasoned ladies who advised him: "It is better to get rid of the trouble of delivery, for you don't know what may be the outcome?" But Dubey ji was not prepared for it. "If this is god's will, let it happen that way."

At last when 12 months had completed to the conception, Hulsi started having very severe labour pains. Eventually on the 7th day of the bright fortnight of the lunar month of Sawan (nearly August), Hulsi delivered a strange child. It was a boy who appeared as big as a five year old, right at birth time. He had all the 32 teeth intact in his mouth and as soon as he was born he uttered the word 'Ram' to everybody's surprise. All the seniors of the village advised Atma Ram to get rid of this bizarre boy. "It is an inauspicious child and his birth may entail great calamity to the entire village. Throw him in the river Yamuna flowing closeby."

Such advices made Atma Ram all the more distressed. He couldn't even celebrate the birth of his first born. Wherever he went he received the counsel: "Get rid of the boy if you desire safety of this region. Else, we will perish in the divine wrath." Little did these people realise that it would be because of this very boy that many would be redeemed from their distress in the times to come.

Atma Ram was a more worried man when he returned home. He went to his wife who had become very pale and weak due to that unusual delivery. The boy was quietly lying in a cradle with eyes wide open as though he was understanding every word of the conversation between his mother and father.

"All advise me to get rid of our boy, but this I can not do. Neither can I keep on withstanding their bitter opposition to my boy's life. I don't know what to do?"

The mother was also disturbed getting the people's advice in general. But resolutely she declared: "No! we won't get rid of him. But don't worry. I will send this boy to my father's place. This way he will live on. Here we will circulate the rumour that we have thrown the boy in the Yamuna."

Then Hulsi asked Dubeji to summon her favourite maid Chunia. It was she who had helped Hulsi deliver the boy safely. As she was near the boy, she said: "Congratulations, Hulsi Ji. It seems you have given birth to an incarnation of some great deity. I have seen many newly born but never so big a boy with full teeth set. He is no ordinary boy." Since Chunia was sympathetic to the boy, Atma Ram Dubey quickly sent for her. As she reached Hulsi asked her: "Chunia dear! Help us in hour of distress. All the people of this village want my boy murdered. I request you to quietly take this boy to my father's village. There you may hand over this boy to my brother's wife with this letter. I have explained everything in this letter to my Bhabhi. In a day or two, as soon as I become moveable, I will also join you there."

It was quiet late in the night that Atma Ram Dubey sent Chunia with the boy disguised as a cloth-bundle in a bullock cart. Now the father was somewhat relieved. At least a way had been found to avoid the villagers' wrath and let the boy survive.

But his relief was short-lived. The next morning when his wife didn't get up, he yelled at her, but no response. She was dead! Hulsi's death unnerved Atma

Ram greatly. He was now convinced that the boy's birth was indeed inauspicious for the family. He now even feared facing his son. So, instead of going to his in-laws place to meet his new-born son, he left for pilgrimage, as if to atone for sins he might have committed, since he took his inauspicious son's birth as a consequence of his unknown sins.

Meanwhile, Chunia continued to rear up that inauspicious boy quite affectionately even though the news had been received about the death of Hulsi. Although Hulsi's brother, mother and father kept on being afraid of the boy and would scrupulously avoid even seeing his face early in the morning, Chunia kept on playing the role of a doting mother to the unfortunate child. The boy had not been given a name and was often referred to as a jinxed existence. But surprisingly, that little boy, even in his infancy, kept on tolerating all the unconcealed hostility towards him with complete non-chalance. He had become a quiet and timid boy who would keep on gazing at the blank sky without uttering a sound; even without uttering a cry. The only word he ever uttered was 'Ram'. It was only Chunia who detected a definite spark of divinity in him and kept on treating the boy with loving affection. At times she would even take up cudgels with the senior members of the house for the sake of that unusual infant. But God appeared to be quite unkind to the boy. When he was barely five, Chunia also died, leaving the boy unprotected and lonely in that hostile world. Soon the boy was thrown out of the house. Like a vagabond that orphan began to beg at door to door for survival.[1] It is said that only a brahman woman used to offer him some food to help the boy keep his body and soul together. [Some versions claim that - the woman was no other but Goddess Parvati in disguise].

Once it so happened that—perhaps propelled by God's grace—the pet disciple of Shree Anantanandaji Maharaj who resided in a place called 'Ram-shel'. Shree Naraharyananda happened to visit that village. He happened to spot this five year old boy sitting quietly before a temple for hours together. He took the boy under his care when he learnt about the wretched life he was leading. It was he who gave 'Ram-Bola' name to that boy who uttered only Ram's name. ['Ram-Bola' literally means one who utters Ram's name]. Then Naraharyananda took that boy to Ayodhya. It was in the year 1504 that the Swami arranged for the boy's sacred thread ceremony. It is customary that during this ceremony the brahman boys are initiated in pronouncing the most sacred 'Gayatri Mantra'. While Naraharyananda was about to initiate 'Ram-Bola' into pronouncing the sacred mantra, the boy surprised everyone by uttering the mantra with perfect pronunciation! Now the Swami was convinced that the boy was an extraordinary soul. 'Else, how could he

---

1. Writing about his early life, Tulsidas says in his 'Kavitavali':

"Matu-pita jag jehi tajyo vidihee na likhee kachhu bhaal bhalayee." [Discarded by the parents and disowned by the world, I had no hope of bright future since Brahma had ordained nothing good for me.]

pronounce the Gayatri Mantra so perfectly when he is as yet unable to read or write,' the swami thought. Mightily impressed by the boy's extraordinary precocity, he also initiated Ram-Bola to his precious 'Ram-Mantra' after completing all the five childhood 'sanskaras' of the boy. Then he made the boy learn about the various sacred texts and taught him to read and write. The boy learnt all that he was taught in no time. He had the ability of repeating verbatim all that his Guru taught him. Having stayed in Ayodhya for sometime, Naraharyananda took him to Soron (a place in Badayun district, on the banks of river Ganga). It was here that the boy, 'Ram-Bola' heard the 'Rama-Tale' for the first time. Here the boy would also assist his Guru in the public recitation of the sacred text. He became quite deft in public speaking as well. After passing many years in Soron, Naraharyananda went to Kashi (Varanasi) with the boy. He had his education completed in Kashi.

Creation of the 'Hanuman-Chalisa'

While studying under the guidance of his guru with other disciples, the boy, 'Ram-Bola' found in him the art of rhyming even without much effort. He would often regale his friends with his little poems made on the spot. But despite of all his abilities the boy was rather chicken-hearted. He would fear beasts and other animals and even the very mention of ghosts would scare him out of his wits. When the guru learnt about his weakness he advised him to concentrate his mind on Lord Hanuman, the despoiler of all fear. Since that day he became a devotee of Lord Hanuman.

One day when his friends were mocking at his chicken-heartedness, 'Ram-Bola' told them that by the grace of Lord Hanuman he had now become totally fearless. They, then, challenged him to light the lamp of the temple of Lord Hanuman situated amidst very eerie surroundings close to a dilapidated crematorium on the banks of the river Ganga. Ram-Bola's friends offered him the bait of bellyful 'Rabari' if he could light the lamp in the temple after the sun-set. Ram-Bola accepted the challenge.

As the sun-set, the friends asked Ram-Bola to go to the temple. It was biting cold and it was a moonless night. Ram-Bola summoned enough courage while his friends cheered him up to complete the task. He began to climb the ladders to the temple. As he stepped on the very first step a strong draught of the wind unnerved him, and as if out of reflex action a line of verse emerged from his mouth:

"*Jai Hanuman*[1] *gyan guna sagar*!"

The invisible presence of Lord Hanuman seemed to make him retain his composure. By that time a slight drizzle had also started. Shivering in his raggish clothes, he climbed on to the second step while chanting Lord Hanuman's name: "*Jai Kapees tihun lok ujagar.*"

In this way he kept on composing each line of his juvenile poem. When he reached the final step - the

---

1. The entire text of this poem popularly called the 'Hanuman-Chalisa' is given in the translation section with its Hindi and English translation.

40th one - to the temple, he had not only won the bet but had also completed his poem now renowned as the Hanuman Chalisa.

This event made the boy particularly devoted to Lord Hanuman. When he returned triumphantly to enjoy a tasty meal of 'Rabari' the feeling of fear was history for his personality.

Tulsidas, till now Ram-Bola, continued to stay with his guru Swami Naraharyananda, till he was fifteen. When he had completed his education, he longed for visiting his native place, the village Rajapur. The guru permitted him.

But when he returned home he found it totally in ruins. His father Atmaram was long dead. In fact when Ram-Bola reached his native village nobody recognised him. He had never lived there previously, being driven out of the village at his very birth. Even for him Rajapur was a strange village. He had to give his long introduction to the villagers to make them agree to his staying in the village. As a matter of fact, there were some of his cousins who still remembered his inauspicious birth and the subsequent disintegration of Atmaram Dubey's family. They were reluctant to let Ram-Bola stay in the village but the senior members of the Dubey community allowed him to stay as they knew that Ram-Bola was the only son of Atmaram Dubey.

Having received the permission to stay in the village, Ram-Bola cleared his dilapidated house and made it a little dwelling place. But opposition to him, owing to his being an auspicious child continued to surface frequently. It was only when Ram-Bola had passed some days in the village that people began to accept him. After all he was much more learned than any other member of the village. He had received his education in Kashi and had the ability to recite 'Katha' with great effect. Adding to this quality was his sweet voice. He would often lapse in a musical rendering of the Katha. Gradually he became popular in the village. His 'Katha-recital' was truly captivating. He would recite to the villagers the tales from the sacred books with great command over the language. He had a penchant for explaining the thoughts expressed in terse Sanskrit in the most captivating, easy to comprehend, local language. Soon he became a renowned 'katha vachaka' in the region. His fame not only made him more acceptable but it also started to provide him a source of wherewithal. With the house re-established and food twice in a day assured from various houses, Ram-Bola started to dwell there peacefully.

Ram Bola had a captivating personality - very fair complexion, shining eyes, long ears and a robust body developed through exercises and daily swimming, first in the Ganga and now in the Yamuna, Ram-Bola's youthful body could entice any girl. Now he also started feeling the urge for female company. Ram-Bola thought it was time he married. He was now in the prime of youth and a renowned, self-sufficient brahman of high predigree. He started getting many offers for marriage. At last on 13th lunar day of the bright fortnight of the year Samvat 1583 (1527 AD) he was married to Ratnavali, the daughter of a brahman of repute of the gotra Bhardwaj. Following the marriage he began to live peacefully with his comely wife.

This was, actually a period of total distraction for Ram-Bola. He forgot about his worship and began to live almost inseparably close to his wife. Often he used to be the butt of ridicule of his friends for his uncontrollable love for his wife. Ram-Bola found himself helpless to control his urge for intimacy for various psychological reasons. He had no brothers or sisters; no recollection of his parents and had only a faint memory of Chunia. Before he got married he was virtually alone in the entire world. Now in Ratna he found someone who could be called his own. Moreover, after years of neglect and isolation, he had someone to talk and love. He would not let Ratnavali leave him for a second. Even his schedule of reciting Katha at various places appeared to him a great distraction. Of course, he would continue to complete his schedule of Katha recital and worship, but with great reluctance. His popularity also began to decline. But unmindful, Ram-Bola continued to remain infatuated to his wife Ratnavali.

Ratnavali was also in a fix. No doubt she was a loving wife and would succumb to her husband's desires, even after a couple of months when she detected no reduction in her husband's infatuation, she decided to go to her mother's place. The month of Sawan had started and it was customary for the newly married girls to visit their mother's place. Her brother had already come to invite her. Her mother's place was not far, just across the river. But Ram-Bola was reluctant to let her go. He gave many excuses in order to keep Ratnavali with him. But his brother-in-law also explained things to him. Eventually after much cajoling and coaxing, he agreed to let Ratnavali go for a short duration to her mother's place. Ratnavali thought that possibly her absence might make her husband realise his mistake. So, promising to return soon, Ratnavali left with her brother to go to her mother's place.

3

Wife's Admonition, Turns Ram-Bola Into Tulsidas

After Ratnavali's departure Ram-bola felt as though his life had become a burden. Every time he decided to read the sacred text or devote some time in reading the Ramayana, he found Ratnavali's comely physique coming before his eyes. He tried to prepare food for himself but left it half cooked as he found no appetite. 'How could I pass the time during her absence' was the thought that kept troubling him. No matter what he did he found Ratnavali's face staring at him from all quarters. At last he decided to take bath in the river. But reaching the river he longed to cross it and go to Ratna's place that was not far from the other bank of the river. He even enquired from one or two boatmen but they said: " The river is in high spate and it is not safe to go. By the time we return it would be dark and we may be stranded on the other bank". He returned home after taking a casual bath. Though he tried to concentrate on his ritual worship of Lord Ram he found it beyond him. All the time he kept on thinking about Ratna, 'May be she is also longing for my company now. Should I go across swimming?' He kept on toying with the idea but couldn't decide. He also feared the taunt that he might have to face if he reached close to Ratna that very day itself. Lost in the vortex of indecision Ram-Bola didn't go to recite the Katha in the nearby hamlet. When the persons from that hamlet came he pretended his inability due to illness. It had become dark and Ram-Bola kept on lying on his cot beholding mentally whatever Ratna might be doing at that time in her mother's house. Right since his marriage he had passed no night without Ratna. It was really getting unbearable. At last he decided to go to Ratna that very night.

As he set out of his house, it had started to rain. But undaunted, he kept on proceeding towards the river bank, facing slush and grime caused by the intensifying rain. He had become totally wet but his resolve to meet Ratna was still firm. When he reached the bank of the river, he found not a soul there. The sky had started pouring heavily and there was no boat in sight. Still he waded through the water. The current was fast and strong. It was becoming difficult for him to maintain his desired direction. Though he was an expert swimmer he found it rather difficult to make even an inch's progress towards the desired destination. While he was frantically moving his hands and feet, he found a floating raft touching his hand. Using it as the support he kept on floating and swimming alternately to gain some respite from the fast current. Twice he appeared to have been drowned in a whirlpool but he managed to get out of it due to his sheer robustness. After much difficulty he crossed the mid-current and reached the other bank of the river. As he approached the bank, a severe lightening flash lit the entire area. In a flash he saw that the 'raft' was nothing else but a floating dead body.' A chilling wave ran down his spine and quickly he thrust the body aside. Now, he was in knee-deep water and wading through it he reached the dry land. Resting for a while beneath a tree he proceeded toward Ratna's house which was about a couple of miles due east.

Now he began to walk quickly, imagining Ratna's enthusiastic welcome to his heroic deed! Little did he know what lay in store for him!

It was quite dark but a flash of lightning made him locate Ratna's house. He reached before it only to find all doors closed from inside. Though he knocked at the gates and yelled for Ratna, the noise of the pelting rain and swelling wind drowned his voice. Getting no response he moved around the house searching for an opening . He found a tree high enough to touch the balcony of the house. He quickly climbed the tree. Fortunately he found a sort of thick rope hanging from the sill of a window. Though he found the rope quite slippery he managed to grab it firmly and reached the window. As he reached the window,[1] he shuddered in fright once again. What he thought to be a rope was actually a thick and sturdy python, this he could see in the flash of yet another spell of lightning which also

1. The whole sequence of this journey has been described in a folk-bhajan believed to have been penned by Tulsidas himself which is given at the end of the translation-section.

made him see Ratna lying on the cot inside the room behind the window. He was delighted. His hazardous journey had brought him to the right point of his destination. He quickly thrust open the partially open window and jumped through it inside the room. Then reaching near the cot he said in a muted voice: "Ratna-Ratna . . I have come!"

Ratna was shocked to hear a muted voice emerging from such a close quarter. She was not in a deep sleep. She quickly got up and enhanced the glow of a burning lamp kept closeby. Ram-bola again said: "Ratna-Ratna!.. It is me, Ram-Bola", and he tried to madly embrace his wife. Ratna was amazed and was left agape for a few seconds.

"Who....., Yoooooou!" She couldn't believe it.

"No one else, Dear! I couldn't pass even one night without you. Crossing the swelling river and moving on a treacherous path, I have come before you at last!" Ram-Bola said with an air for his achievement. But Ratna's reaction was totally unexpected.

"Fie upon you! You, a lecherous fellow! You have no sense. You are a mad man. How could you come here? What would my brother and Bhabhi say when they learn that you came here in this fashion. I thought you to be a learned fellow but you appear to be worse than an animal. Now get away quickly before other members of the house know about your trespassing into the house in this way!"

Ram-Bola was speechless for a second! "Are all these words being uttered, directed towards him? Why is she not appreciating my effort to meet her? Am I an animal? She says: fie upon me!" Ram-Bola was bewildered.

Then Ratna again admonished him. "So much of love you have for my this fey body? Why don't you concentrate your mind on God[1]. Even half of this kind of love for Ram would have redeemed you from all mundane distresses. Don't be a lecherous insect! Be a man and love God. Only then you shall be free from all mundane worries. Now, go away! I don't want anybody to see you here!"

Ram-Bola was stung to the quick. Ratna's incisive words had pierced his heart. He was speechless for some time. And then he spoke in a measured tone:

"Ratna! Thanks for guiding me towards my right destination. You have now converted a plant of Bhang[2] into the plant of the holy basil. Henceforth, Ram-Bola would be known as Tulsidas. Now I leave you and shall never come to your bed. You are now my god-mother for you have shown me the correct path. I leave you now for ever. Good-bye!"

---

1. The Doha she said at this occasion is quoted verbatim below:

Asthi-charm maya deha mum
Tā men eisse preeti!
Jo hoti Raghunath prati, tau ne hoti
bhava-bheeti!

[Had you loved Lord Ram with the same devotion as you have shown to my this body made of bones and skin, perhaps we have had no fear in our mortal life].

2. This simile Tulsidas uses in Ramcharitmanas's Doha given ahead in the translation section no. 120.

Ratna realised that perhaps she had over-reacted. She knew her 'Ram-Bola', a man of strong resolve. She quickly said:" Don't be so hurt. I said all this for your welfare. I know your capabilities. You are destined to shine like a star. I want to see you famous and renowned. Promise that you will come once to me before I leave this world."

Tulsidas, a changed man, said: "That I shall do. Now good-bye!"

While this discussion was taking place, other members of the house also got up. They tried to impress upon Tulsi to stay put at least for the rest of the night. But he would not agree. Keeping quiet, with a resolute determination writ large on his face, he left Ratna's house there and then.

While coming out of the house in total quietude, Tulsi's heart was as disturbed as a sea in storm. But, amazingly, he was feeling no rancour for Ratna. On the contrary, he was feeling a sense of gratitude for Ratna. To Tulsidas it appeared as though he was coming out of a nightmare of sensual infatuation. As the sun dawned he felt a sublime peace and he started singing:

"Kāhe na Tulsi Rām kaho re!"

His prowess in poetry was now shining. The goddess of speech, Saraswati, was shedding her benign grace as he crossed the river in a boat to go back to his native place. He felt relieved and revived. The poet in him was wide awake. Ram-Bola, a captive of sensual attraction had given way to Tulsidas, the poet with a vision of universality. The transformation was quick and sharp.

4

Tulsidas Turns Into an Ascetic Devoted to Lord Ram

Reaching his village he took all the essential things and wore a saffron ensemble to declare his embracing the ascetic order. The villagers were surprised seeing such a gay cavilier boy, captive to the sensual delights, becoming an ascetic almost overnight. Although they asked him to wait for Ratna's return, Tulsidas said: "It is she who has made me now whatever I am. She is my guru and it is at her bidding that I have become an ascetic. But my relationship with her hasn't been snapped, it has only been changed."

And saying so, he left his native village to become part of the universe. His identification was not confined to his being a dweller of Rajapur for he had seemingly developed a communion with eternity. He left on a long pilgrimage to cleanse the remaining mundane filth in his heart. First he went to Prayag. There he met many Saadhus in whose company he started visiting all the holy spots. Travelling with them he also visited

Mansarovar whose cool quietude filled his heart with a serene bliss. It is claimed that at Mansarovar he met the ageless crow, Kakubhushandi- who had personally witnessed the age of Ram - and who further initiated Tulsi into the 'bhakti' of Ram. From there, seeing many pilgrim centres on the way, he returned to Kashi. Sitting in a small hut on the banks of the river Ganga, Tulsidas, began to recite Katha of Ram to the desirous devotees. Since he was adept in reciting the story with musical interpretations, he soon started having a considerable audience. Every time, after concluding his recital beneath a banyan tree, he would pour the holy water from the Kamandal on to the root of that tree.

One day, late in the night when he poured the holy water after the conclusion of the recital as was his routine, he was baffled to hear a voice speaking from the top of the tree, "Blessed be thy life, O ascetic! For your pouring water on to the root of this tree had satisfied my thirst. I have now been redeemed from my this state."

Unable to locate the source of the voice, Tulsidas asked: "Who are you? I can't see you."

"I am a ghost. In my previous life I was a brahman who indulged in vices with gay abandon. As a consequence of that misdeed I had to become a ghost. But now you have redeemed me from that state. I am prepared to grant you any boon you desire." Binding his hands in reverence, Tulsidas said: "O my benefactor! I am delighted to have been of some help to you even though unconsciously. Thank you for the boon offer.

The only boon I seek is this: Can you make me more devoted to my chosen Lord Ram?"

The ghost expressed his inability as it was beyond his competence. But he said: "Why don't you seek Lord Hanuman's guidance for this purpose? "Where can I get Lord Hanuman? I know that only he is competent to do so. But how to reach him? I have been an ardent devotee to Lord Hanuman as well, right since my childhood but I am yet to get his blessings!"

Then the ghost confided in him. "You must have seen a leper coming to attend your Katha recital. He always sits in the farthest corner, but he is always first to reach the venue and leave it after all have left. Now when you spot him, fall flat on his feet. May be he sheds his benign grace onto you. In fact he is present in every gathering where the Ram-Katha is recited."

Tulsidas was thrilled to learn about Lord Hanuman in disguise listening to the Ram-katha recited by him. Now he was on the look-out for that evasive 'leper.'

Next evening when the katha was about to commence Tulsidas spotted that leper. Even in his wildest dreams he couldn't have imagined that leper to have been Lord Hanuman in disguise. Thanking profusely to that ghost who revealed the secret, he decided to meet that leper when the recital was over.

After the conclusion of the Katha when all had left, Tulsidas reached close to that leper who was about to leave. Falling flat at the feet of that leper and bursting into his poem he had created in his childhood he said:

"Jai Hanuman gyan guna sagar!"

The leper was visibly annoyed. He said: "Hey you! Get away from me. Else you may also be stricken with this dreadful disease. And why are you addressing me this way. I am a leper and no one else."

Now Tulsidas caught hold of that leper's feet firmly, " No, lord! I know who you are! You are no one else but the chief devotee of Lord Ram - you are Lord Hanuman!" Although that leper tried his best to deter Tulsidas from touching him, eventually he was pleased with Tulsidas's firm devotion and revealed himself. Seeing him in his true form Tulsidas burst into reciting an instantly created Doha of his:

"Lal Deha Lali lasei
Aru dhari lal langoor |
Vaja deh danav dalan
Jai jai jai Kapi shoor!!

[Red is your complexion and red is your tail lying there. Your body is as strong as the thunderbolt - I bow to you repeatedly - O bravest of the apes!].

Lord Hanuman benignly smiled and said: "Get up Tulsi. Lord Ram has sent you to me. We both have one mission: Spread the glories of Lord Ram."

Tulsidas again bowed to him and said: "Lord! How can I have the Darshan of Lord Ram? Please guide me to him."

Lord Hanuman said: "You better go to Chitrakoot[1]. There you might get his Darshan and he disappeared.

Tulsidas was thrilled. Now he had had the Darshan of Lord Hanuman and by his grace might also see Lord Ram. Mentally describing the virtues of Lord Hanuman he started to create a poem.

Reaching back his hut he immediately bound his belongings into a cloth bundle and left for Chitrakoot. Reaching there, he stayed at the Ramghat. After a few days when he was returning to his hut after completing his morning ritual worship, he spotted two very comely and strong princes going astride two brilliant steeds. Believing them to have been sons of a powerful king, he didn't pay any special attention to them.

But that very night Lord Hanuman appeared in his dream and said: "Tulsi! Now your ardent wish must have been fulfilled. Lord Ram with his younger brother Lakshman had appeared before you seated on sturdy horses!"

Tulsidas was shocked: "Oh! So, those two princes were my chosen Lord Ram and his brother Lakshman! How unfortunate have I been! I couldn't recognise them, nor did I bow to them, deeming them to be some secular princes!" Tulsidas began to repent for having missed that rare opportunity. Then he requested Lord

1. A holy spot in modern M.P. not far from Rewa. The Ramayana says that this was the place where Bharat met Ram during the latter's exile.

Hanuman. "Please, Lord, allow me to have a fleeting glimpse of them once more. This time I shall be doubly alert."

Lord Hanuman then reassured Tulsidas that the following morning he would see the Lord. Next morning when Tulsidas was sitting on the stairs of the Ramghat and grinding sandal paste for his worship ritual, he suddenly found two very brilliant princes reaching him and demanding a bit of the sandal paste. In order to ensure that Tulsi might not miss this opportunity of recognising his chosen Lord, Lord Hanuman, disguised as a parrot sitting on the branch of a closeby tree, recited the following Doha:

Chitrakoot ke ghat par

bhayee santan kee bheer |

Tulsidas chandan ghisen

Tilak deta Raghuveer ||

[Amidst the large crowd of the holy men in Chitrakoot, while Tulsidas was grinding sandalwood to convert it into the paste form, Raghuveer appeared before him demanding the paste to mark his forehead].

Beholding that superb vision of Lord Ram marking his forehead with the paste and also applying a little of it at his own forehead, Tulsidas was lost in a trance. He forgot all about his body; he had no awareness of time and space. He was totally lost in that vision, and by the time he was wide awake, there was nothing before him but that ghat of Chitrakoot. But Tulsidas was ecstatic. "What holy saints receive after eons of their devoted worship has now been received by me by Lord Hanuman's grace. Blessed is my life and Great is Lord Ram". That vision so much influenced Tulsidas that for coming many days he was not normal. That Doha uttered by Hanumanji in the parrot's form kept on ringing in his ears, and with that haunting Doha he kept on seeing Lord Ram's visage!

One day Hanumanji again appeared in his dreams and asked Tulsidas to go to Ayodhya. Obeying the instructions, Tulsi left Chitrakoot and reached Prayag, but at that time the famous Magh Mela of Prayag was on. So he stayed for some days in that holy congregation of the holy saints.

It is said that in that mela he also met the famous saints who are copiously referred to in mythological accounts, viz. sage Yagyavalkya and sage Bharadwaj, seated beneath the immortal Banyan Tree.[1] There the Ram-katha was being recited the similar way as Tulsi had heard in his childhood at Soron Kshetra. Hearing that tale he was further inspired to write it in his own words.

From Prayag, Tulsi went to Kashi. While there staying with a brahman at Prahlad Ghat he felt like rendering that famous tale in his own words in Sanskrit. He started to compose verse in Sanskrit, but a peculiar phenomenon took place. All the verses that he composed in Sanskrit in the entire day would be found missing the following morning. Even though Tulsi took

1. This fabled tree is still very much in existence. It is said to be immortal because its age has never been deciphered.

great care to preserve his verses he couldn't find as to who stole them. This process continued for more than a week. Then one night he found Lord Shankar appearing in his dream and asking him to compose the Ram-katha in the commonly understood language of the period.

[Of course, this divine inspiration-story, as is available in all the accounts recording Tulsidas's life, might be true but the fact cannot be denied that Tulsidas himself had seen through the game of the Sanskrit interpreters who invariably translated the sacred text suiting to their own communal bias. Perhaps in order to make the common man realise the truth that lay in the sacred text that Tulsidas opted for writing this adored tale in the '*lingua franca*' of the time].

This divine inspiration through a dream made Tulsidas wake up from his sleep. It was almost middle of the night. Then, as the authentic accounts on Tulsi's life-story aver, Tulsidas also saw Lord Shankar appearing before him and asking him to rewrite the entire tale of Rama in the commonly understood language which was an admixture of various dialects of Hindi, viz. Braja-Bhashya, Avadhi, Bhojpuri, a part of Rajasthani and a part of Malawi. The critics say that at that time the peripatetic mendicants had developed their own typical language called 'Saddhukkharee' (or the language of the Saadhus). It was basically this language that Tulsi adopted for composing his verses.

It is also claimed that Lord Shankar had also advised him to go to Ayodhya and create the epic 'Sri ramcharit manas'. Following the divine instructions Tulsi left for Ayodhya in the beginning of 1575 AD.

5

Tulsi Creats His 'Magnum Opus'

When Tulsidas reached Ayodhya the winter season was at its peak. But this holy town was getting crowded with the devotees coming from all over the country because it was claimed by the renowned astrologers that in that year the holy day of Lord Ram's birth was falling in an identical planetary combination as was witnessed when Ram's birth had actually taken place. It was with much difficulty that Tulsi could get a small hut on the bank of the river Sarayoo. He had to share that hut with one more ascetic-poet from the Vraja-Kshctra, called Nanda Das.[1]

Tulsi started dwelling there. Now he was mentally reconciled to writing the Ram-katha in the local language, but for that he had to prepare himself mentally. It was for this purpose that he started visiting

1. He was the same poet who became one of the renowned poets of the 'Ashtha-Chhaap' school. It was during this stay that Nanda Das grew very affectionate with Tulsidas and on whose invitation Tulsi had visited Vraja Kshetra where he met Soordas. The details about that meeting are given in our book 'Soordas' of the same series.

every place of the town associated with Lord Ram. He would go out every day to visit the famous spots like the place of the birth, Sarayoo Ghat, Hanuman Garhi, etc.

Tulsi wanted to absorb the entire ambience of the region before setting to writing the renowned tale in verse. Since the major familial upheaval of this tale had taken place in Ayodhya following Lord Rama's exile, he started to compose first the 'Ayodhya-kanda' and not from the beginning.

He commenced composing his famous epic 'Sri ramcharita manas' exactly on the 'RAM- NAVAMI DAY' of the Samvat 1631. He began composing it with great devotion. But, having heard about his intention of writing the Ram-katha in the lingua franca of the time, he started facing a lot of trouble from the local pundits. They did not doubt Tulsidas's prowess in Sanskrit and they also knew that Tulsidas's purpose was to reveal the entire essence of the sacred text in an easy to follow language. This endangered the Sanskrit pandits,' thus far unassailable, position as the sole interpreters of the Hindu religious text. So, when Tulsidas completed his 'Ayodhaya kanda' its only copy available was stolen. It is believed that at the benest of the local pundits the goons had stolen the copy and had thrown it into the Sarayoo river. It was a sad blow to Tulsidas. Yet, undaunted, he started to rewrite it from memory. Again an attempt was made to steal it. But when the goons reached near Tulsidas's hut in the middle of the night to steal his creation of the 'Ayodhya Kanda', to their utter surprise, they found two young lads guarding the hut. By their description it was revealed that they were no one else but Ram and Lakshman themselves.

Tulsidas was delighted to know that his creation stood approved by his chosen Lord and hence His safeguarding it but he was also sorry to realise that because of him his Lord had to be disturbed.

Nevertheless, with all these disturbances and man-made troubles he kept on writing his 'Manas'. He would also recite it to learn the common people's reaction to it. They were thrilled. They had never heard the Ram-Katha in such an engrossing style. The book, though it was not yet complete, began to earn the people's admiration. Every evening, for some time Tulsidas used to recite some portions from it and the people loved it. As a result, his audience began to swell in size progressively.

Tulsidas had written it in a unique style. He would start the new canto with an invocation of various gods and goddesses in Sanskrit and then would lapse into the commonly understood language. Even his Sanskrit pieces are masterpieces which shut the mouth of those Sanskrit pundits who had spread rumours that Tulsi wrote in the 'boorish' language because he had no command over Sanskrit. Not only the Sanskrit pundits of Ayodhya but even of Kashi saw Tulsidas as their potential rival. But no matter how villainous were their attempts to belittle importance of Tulsidas's creation, the fame of his monumental work 'Sri ramcharita manas' began to spread far and wide even before it was complete. It is said that it took two years, seven months and twenty six days for Tulsidas to complete it. Exactly on the day Lord Ram married - that is in the bright fortnight of the month Margsheersha (late November) - in the year Samvat 1633, that it was duly completed in all respects.

Since Tulsidas had written it from the divine inspiration he received from Lord Vishwanath, (Lord Shankar) in Kashi, he thought it should be placed first in the temple of Lord Vishwanath in Kashi. So with his creation safely lying in his hands, he left for Kashi. Reaching there he recited the whole of it in the temple in his own voice for a couple of days and in order to get divine approval it was left in the temple for the night. Next morning when the temple was opened and the tome was taken out all were baffled to see. "Satyam Shivam Sundaram[1]", written on its first page followed by Lord Shanker's emblem - the Trishool's - imprint. The great Lord had whole-heartedly approved it'. It is said that a mysterious voice continued to resound when the temple was opened that morning: "Satyam Shivam Sundaram"!

Tulsidas was delighted. His attempt had been a spectacular success. While many people came to congratulate it, there were also those diehard pundits who turned green with envy at Tulsidas's success. They again began to spread a vicious canard against Tulsidas. They said: "This fellow Tulsi is not even a brahman it appears! For no brahman would write in such a cheap

1. Perfect in all respects.

language. He has wrongly interpreted our sacred text. Moreover, he has made the pithy meaning of the sacred text available even for the lowly born shoodras. They are not entitled to have access to this supreme knowledge. This book is sure to disturb our social fabric; it would be irreparably torn by this boorish language interpretations, etc."

However, no matter what they did they couldn't help check the growing popularity of 'Sriramcharita manas' and of Tulsidas. Right from princes to paupers all longed to read it, but, the villainous pundits were still hatching conspiracies to destroy the book.

Since it was not the age when a manuscript could be converted into a thousand copies overnight, the manuscript had to be kept guarded. But Tulsidas never cared to protect it. He thought it to be the god's work and was sure that unless the gods desired so, it would never be destroyed. But he had not thought about his human enemies. The group of the jealous pundits again made two expert thieves steal it and then destroy it. The thieves went to Tulsidas's hut and in the depth of night when Tulsidas fell asleep they tried to clandestinely enter the hut with the intention of stealing the manuscript. But again they found two handsome lads with bows and arrows in their hands guarding the hut. That vision not only prevented them from making any attempt to break into the hut but also changed their heart as much as to make them become Tulsidas's followers. They themselves disclosed this conspiracy of the villianous pundits.

Tulsidas was quite sad knowing about the theft attempt once again. He felt quite embarrassed that his creation was repeatedly disturbing his chosen Lord and forcing him to stand guard to his manuscript. He even thought of destroying it but people protested violently against this view. They said "this rare gem has to be preserved at all costs. It is the emperor's responsibility to ensure its safety".

When this public opinion was conveyed to the royal court of Akbar, Todarmal, a good friend of Tulsidas and one of the nine gems of the court of Akbar, was deputed to ensure the manuscript's safety. Tulsidas happily entrusted the manuscript of his 'Manas' to Todarmal's custody and made another copy of it himself. It was from the second copy that hundreds of the copies of 'Sriramcharita manas' began to be made. It was growing increasingly popular and began to be treated, already, as the sacred book of the Hindus.

But the villainous group of the jealous pundits was still hatching conspiracies to deride the book. When they couldn't do much, they asked Madhusoodan Saraswati, the most revered Sanskrit scholar of that time in Kashi, to read the 'Manas' and give his final verdict. Since they thought that Madhusoodan Saraswati, being a Sanskrit scholar, was sure to criticise the book written in the language of the villagers, using his opinion they would spread their canard against Tulsidas more effectively. But to their utter surprise, Madhusoodan Saraswati went through that book and expressed his verdict by means of a Sanskrit Shloka:

"Ananadakaanani Hyaismajangams Tulasi Taruh |
Kavita Manjari Bhati Rambhramar Bhoosita"||

[If Kashi is a lovely garden giving bliss, Tulsidas is a mobile Tulsi (basil) plant. The pollen of that plant is that superior poetry over which the captivated bee in the form of Lord Ram ever circles].

This candid and final opinion from a renowned Sanskrit pundit failed the scheming pundits of Kashi and they thought of yet another trick to malign Tulsidas's work. Now they came up with the plea that let Lord Vishwanath decide as to what should be the status of the 'Sriramcharita manas' among all the sacred books. They connived with the priest of the renowned Vishwanath Temple and had all the sacred books of the Hindu faith placed before the idol of Vishwanath including the 'Manas' in such a way that the 'Manas' came to be placed at the bottom of all the sacred tomes. So this creation of Tulsidas was placed under the four Vedas, all the Puranas, Upanishads and other books of the same genre. Then the temple gate was closed for the night. When in the morning the temple gate was opened the pundits found to their great chagrin the 'Sriramcharita manas' placed upon all the sacred texts. It was almost the definitive opinion of the Lord. Now the pundits had to go to apologise before Tulsidas and accept his 'Manas' as the most important book for Hindu faith. They even washed Tulsidas's feet reverentially and offered to drink that water in which his feet had been washed. But Tulsidas prevented them from doing so with the magnanimous comment: "Well it is entirely His creation and I am merely an instrument to pen it down at the Lord's bidding. I am a humble devotee of Lord Ram and I do all that he commands me to do." Nevertheless, this episode finally accorded the importance the 'Manas' deserved. Ever since its popularity, has been steadily increasing and now it is treated at par with even those holy books that were revealed by Lord Almighty Himself. Tulsidas still stands as a peerless poet of the literature of all times.

6

Tulsidas And Emperor Akbar

It has already been mentioned that Todarmal, one of the 'gems' of Emperor Akbar's court was a good friend of Tulsidas. His 'Manas' was considered such a priceless treasure that on public demand it was preserved in Todarmal's treasury. Tulsidas was also quite friendly with other members of the emperor's court. One of them was Birbal who was also a poet in his own right. The other friend and well-wisher of Tulsidas in Akbar's court was the famous poet, Abdur-Rahim 'Khankhana', whose poems and dohas written under the pseudonym 'Rahim' are still quite popular. In fact, as the records of that age reveal, Tulsidas used to have a sort of regular correspondence with Rahim, but their correspondence also was quite poetic. Rahim was a renowned scholar of Braja-Bhasha, Sanskrit, Hindi and Persian-Arabic and was also well known for charitable disposition. He had helped many poets including Tulsidas in their hour of distress. The budding poets used to receive even gold coins in return of reciting their good couplets before Rahim. But Rahim never felt proud of his position or knowledge. Once, it is said, Tulsidas asked him as to why he never looked into the eye of the person whom he benefited by his liberal charity, and Rahim's famous, humble, reply was:

"Dena har koi aur hai deta diwas aur rain!

Log bharam hum par karen tate neeche nain||"

[The fact is, it is not I but someone else (god) who is the real bestower of the gifts. But since people deem me to be the donor, it is out of sheer shame (of getting the undeserved credit) that I keep my eyes down].

Once Tulsidas sent him one line of a couplet and requested Rahim to complete it. The line was:

"Sura-tiya nar-tiya, naag tiya
Suta chahiyat sab koya!"

[Who is that son whom all the women of gods, men and even the naags (serpents) would like to mother. (In other words, who is the most adorable son for the women of all species) and pat came the answer from Rahim,

"Goda liyen Hulasi phiren
Tulsi so suta hoya"

[He is Tulsidas whom his mother Hulsi carries in her lap in apparent pride and delight.]

Akbar's Confrontation With Tulsidas

Once on the invitation of Nanda Das, Tulsidas happened to come to visit Vraja-Kshetra (Mathura Vrindavan etc.). During this visit he also met the other great poet of Medieval times, Soordas[1]. While Soordas chose Lord Krishna, Tulsidas's was Lord Ram.

---

1. This meeting has been described in details in the book 'Soordas' of the same series.

Once while travelling in Mathura-Vrindavana, in the company of Soordas and Nanda Das, the latter two poets found Tulsidas not bowing his head before the idols of Lord Krishna. When questioned, Tulsidas replied, addressing his Doha to Lord Krishna

"Kaha kahon chhabi aapakee
bhale bane ho Nath |
Tulsi mastak tab navei |
Jab dhanush-ban lehu hath ||

[How should I describe your brilliant image O Lord, you look grand. But Tulsi's head would be bowed only when you wield bow and arrow in your hand!]

It is believed that Tulsidas's this exhorting couplet was created viewing the appalling condition of the society in which all norms seemed to have been thrown to dogs due to turbulent condition of the time. That was the reason that Tulsi desired to behold the militant image of the Lord, who could set right all disorders.

*****

After the completion of the 'Manas' Tulsidas had become famous throughout the country. When he visited Mathura, Todarmal requested him to also visit Delhi, the seat of authority then. Tulsidas readily obliged him.

By that time Akbar had also heard about Tulsidas. He asked Todarmal to arrange for his meeting with Tulsidas. Todarmal knew that Tulsidas never visited any king's court. Why should he bow before the mortal kings when he had direct access through his concentration to Lord Almighty? But Todarmal requested him to have an informal meeting with the emperor. He said to Tulsidas: "Treat him as the part of this entire creation which you declare being instinct with Lord Ram and His spouse, Sita. Haven't you written:

'Siya-Ram maya sab jag jaani

Karahun pranam jori jug pani"

[Deeming the entire world instinct with Sita and Ram, I bow before all hand-bound].

Tulsidas smiled and said: "Todarmal! you know the art of defeating a person by using his own argument. All-right, I am ready to meet your emperor".

So, one fine morning accompanied by Todarmal, Tulsidas reached the Deewan-i-Aam to grant his audience to the emperor. Akbar received him with due welcome. And then said: "O Peer[1]! I have heard that you are a man with many hidden powers. You are reputed to be an exalted 'Faqeer'. But I will accept your greatness only when you show me some miracle. Show it to me here!"

Tulsidas replied with a smile: "Samrat! Perhaps you have been misinformed about me. I am no such man who claims to be having many miracles up his sleeve. I am only an ordinary devotee of Lord Ram. I don't claim to have any special powers at my command. I do only what my Lord asks me to do. Since I have no powers I cannot show any miracle."

---

1. Respectable person, senior etc.

But the emperor would not listen. He refused to believe that one could acquire as much fame and respect merely on the strength of his devotion to his chosen Lord. He kept on pressing his demand on Tulsidas to show some miracle and Tulsidas kept on humbly confessing his possessing no such powers. Todarmal was also feeling embarrassed. But he knew his emperor's shortcoming. Once he became adamant on any demand, he was unlikely to budge. While Todarmal was thinking of some via media to redeem Tulsidas from that unpleasant situation, Akbar, suddenly blew up in rage and ordered his personal attendant, "Put him in the prison and keep him imprisoned till he agrees to show some miracle!"

Tulsidas was taken aback but accepted the situation deeming it to be the will of Ram. Todarmal was hurt. Had he known that his emperor would behave in such a juvenile manner, he wouldn't have brought his respected friend, Tulsidas, in the court. But no matter how close Todarmal had been to his emperor he couldn't have openly revolted against the royal order. He privately apologised to Tulsidas and said: "I'd soon find some way to have you released."

But Tulsidas was unperturbed. He said with a smile:

Hui hai vahee jo Ram rachi rakha
Ko keri tarak badhavahi sakha?!

[Only that shall happen which has been ordained by Lord Ram. Why make useless arguments about what should or should not happen].

And so, while Tulsidas was escorted to the royal prison, a dejected Todarmal went back home.

*****

This incident took late in the morning and within a couple of hours, the people of Delhi witnessed an uncanny and quite a frightening spectacle. All of a sudden, hundreds and thousands of monkeys entered the city of Delhi. They seemed to be coming from all directions. People panicked, for there was hardly a roof top or balcony which was not occupied by bands of ferocious looking monkeys. Their targets particularly were the kitchens of all the people. They would attack and elope with whatever eatable they could lay their hands on. That day not one house in Delhi could prepare lunch. When the royal troops tried to shoo away or attack the monkeys, the Hindu population, which deemed monkeys to be representative of their Lord Hanuman, violently protested. But since the monkeys were not sparing any house, with Muslims getting ready to even kill them, tension in the capital rose to explosive proportions. When the matter was reported to the emperor, he was also amazed. He himself saw the unusual spectacle. Delhi was teeming with monkeys of all variety and they seemed to be seizing the capital. He also heard about the tension rising between the Hindu and Muslim populace. Now, this was the last thing that he could risk. The emperor knew that the Hindu-Muslim amity was the basic strength of his empire. Immediately he summoned Todarmal.

"What's the matter Raja Saheb?" asked Akbar,

"What has caused this sudden and massive invasion of the monkeys?"

"Your Highness," replied Todarmal, "This is perhaps the consequence of your arresting Tulsidas for no offence of his. His is a god - realised soul and Lord Hanuman is his protector. I request you to release him immediatly to avoid wrath of Lord Hanuman. Moreover, you have also seen the miracle you wanted Tulsidas to display," Akbar smiled indulgently. He immediately ordered the release of Tulsidas. As Tulsidas came out of the prison unruffled, the emperor himself welcomed him with a huge plate filled with the costliest gems and gold coins, "Sorry, O Peer! I have committed a mistake. You are truly a god - realised soul and a real devotee of your Lord. Please accept this meagre gift from my side!"

Tulsidas said, "Samrat! Nothing happens here which is not willed by Lord Ram!"

But he refused to accept the precious gifts. At last at Todarmal's intervention, he accepted them and gifted them to the temple where he was staying. It is said that with that treasure a temple dedicated to Lord Hanuman was built. That temple still exists near the ring road in Delhi.

Tulsidas returned to Kashi with added glory and fame.

"What is the matter Raja Sahib," asked Akbar. "What has caused this sudden and massive invasion of the monkeys?"

"Your Highness," replied Todarmal, "This is perhaps the consequence of your arresting Tulsidas for no offence of his. He is a god realised soul and Lord Hanuman is his protector. I request you to release him immediately to avoid wrath of Lord Hanuman. Moreover you have also seen the miracle you wanted Tulsidas to display." Akbar smiled benignly. He immediately ordered the release of Tulsidas. As Tulsidas came out of the prison-compound, the emperor himself welcomed him with a huge plate filled with the costliest gems and gold coins. "Sorry, O Great! I have committed a mistake. You are truly a god-realised soul and a real devotee of your Lord. Please accept this meagre gift from my side."

Tulsidas said, "Samrat! Nothing happens here which is not willed by Lord Ram."

But he refused to accept the precious gifts. At last at Todarmal's intervention, he accepted them and gifted them to the temple where he was staying. It is said that with that treasure a temple dedicated to Lord Hanuman was built. That temple still exists near the ring road in Delhi.

Tulsidas returned to Kashi with added glory and fame.

7

His Last Days and Death

When Tulsidas reached Varanasi (Kashi) he had acquired the status of a celebrity. But he continued to stay in his hut at Assi ghat in Varanasi. Now he had also become a social reformer. With his teachings he had managed to considerably reduce the enmity between the followers of Vishnu and Shiv. Often hc would hold the Katha recital wherein all the Hindu gods used to be evenly extolled. He also started a unique feature in Kashi by holding 'Ram-Leelas' at different places. He had selected various localities which individually staged one important event from Lord Ram's life. While one of the localities staged those activities that took place in Lanka, the other was chosen for staging the activities that took place in Dandak-Kanana. Still those localities carry the same name in Varanasi which was given to them for staging the Ram-Leela connected activities. The localities of Lanka and Nak-Kataiyya are the reminder of that period. Nak-Kataiyya is called so because this locality staged the activity in which Shoorpankha's nose was cut, hence, the term 'Nak-Kataiyya.' It was a unique experiment conducted by Tulsidas. Some scholars claim that staging of Ram-Leelas in entire north-India was started with the efforts of Tulsidas only. Tulsidas had become such an important person in Kashi at that time that he came to be recognised as one of the advisers of the ruler of Kashi[1].

However, it was not that Tulsidas had ceased creating verses after the completion of his celebrated 'Ramcharita manas'. It is said that immediately after returning from his trip to Mathura and Vrindavana he had written 'Krishna Geetavali' which is the only book of verse by him that is dedicated to Lord Krishna. It is claimed that in all he had written more than 40 books of verse. The prominent ones among which are *Sriramcharita manas*, *Vinaya Patrika*, *Geetavali*, *Kavitavali*, *Krishna Geetavali*, *Parvati Mangal*, *Janaki Mangal*, *Baravei Ramayana*, *Hanuman Bahuka*, *Ramagya Prashna*, *Vairagya Sandeepani*, *Ramlala-Nahachhoo* and *Tulsi Satsai*. It is said that *Vinaya Patrika* and *Krishna Geetavali* were the creation he penned immediately after his magnum opus, the 'Manas'.

---

1. Ironically, now, nothing written by Tulsidas in his own handwriting is available, let alone his original copy of 'Sri ramcharita manas' or other creations. Even his any hand-written note is not available barring his signatures in the records of the Kashi Naresh (Ruler) at Ramnagar. It is available in the context of a witness of a case of property dispute in which Tulsidas was asked to sign. However, the most authentic version of the 'Manas' is that copy which is kept in the archives of the 'Kashi Nagari Pracharini Sabha.'

There is an interesting legend attached to some of his creations. The legend goes that after his creation of 'Manas' things started improving morally in the society of the time. Perhaps the partial credit should also be given to the stability that was witnessed in the country following Akbar's consolidating his empire and creating a sort of amity between the two large factions - the Hindus and the Muslims- of the society then. But the legend says that the major contribution was made by the 'Manas' which re-established the moral norms in a telling way. This disturbed Kaliyug's designs. Kaliyug, we know, is the age in which we are and according to the Hindu sacred text it is the age of moral decay. When Kaliyug found Tulsidas disturbing its designs it started troubling him personally, Tulsidas got stricken with a variety of diseases. Then on the advice of Lord Hanuman he started writing poems of 'Vinaya'(full of humility) which were later published under one title, *Vinaya Patrika*. Similarly, he was once stricken with the disease now called 'frozen shoulder' in which hands become almost immobile. Then he wrote 'Hanuman Bahuka' as a prayer to Lord Hanuman to protect him from the Kaliyug influence. By this time his creations had become as famous as to be quoted by the kings and paupers alike. Some of the scholars say that even after completing the 'Manas' he kept on improving it continuously till he was alive.

His Last Meeting With Ratnavali

Tulsidas was now an old man. The onset of various diseases had weakened him. But still he had a heavy load of work. Now he was famous and other poets used to come to him for getting their creations improved. Apart from it, he had other duties as well like organising the Ram leelas and rendering counsel to the King of Varanasi as and when desired. He was maintaining his schedule when one day he had an unusual experience.

It was early in the morning. As he got out of the river Ganga after having his bath he saw a young person bowing to him.

"Tulsi-Baba, Ram-Ram!"

"Ram Ram, Bhai!"

"Couldn't you recognise me?" the stranger asked, adding: "I am one of your distant nephews, Suraj. I am coming from Rajapur. I was coming to Kashi when I got the message from Ratna Kaki."

"Ratna-Ratna!" Tulsidas was reminded of his forgotten wife. All of a sudden the form of Ram-bola lying dormant in his personality was wide awake.

"What happened to her? Is she okay?" he asked.

Suraj then gave all the details about Ratna, saying: "She asked me to convey this message to you, 'Time has come to redeem your pledge!"

Tulsidas immediately realised what it meant. 'Ratna must be on her death-bed and I must go to bid her good bye as I had promised'. Immediately he left for Rajapur.

*****

It took him almost ten days to reach Rajapur. Although he had faith in God, yet he was praying: "Hanuman Baba! Please see that she survives till I reach her. Else I will be failing in my duty to my original guide who guided me to you."

He had never visited Rajapur since he left it about 7 to 8 decades ago. It was much changed but his house was still recognisable. He wondered whether Ratna lived there alone. Straight away he reached his ancestral house and knocked at the gate with a pounding heart.

"Who is there?" asked a female voice, totally unfamiliar to him. He said: "I am Tulsidas!" And quickly the gate was opened. A tiny girl; hardly 10 or 12, yelled seeing him:

"Mayee! An old Baba has come. His name is Tulsidas."

As Ratna heard the name she tried to get up from her sick-bed. She knew that Tulsidas was no one else but her Ram-bola. But before she could do so, guided by that girl, Tulsidas reached inside.

"How are you Ratna?" he asked.

"Waiting for you only!" she replied.

Tulsidas found her to be a mere skeleton. Perhaps she had been ailing for many years. Yet she managed to keep her soul and body together only for ensuring his redeeming his pledge. All of a sudden Tulsidas started humming:

"Kahe na Tulsi! Ram kaho re!"

Ratna looked at him and heard him sing the bhajan with rapt attention. But Tulsidas couldn't know when she breathed her last. She died while listening to the bhajan.

Tulsidas quickly arranged for her funeral and returned to Kashi. Though he lived for many years yet every morning after his bath in the river he would sing the same bhajan.

It was on Saturday, the third lunar day of the dark half of the month of Sawan that Tulsidas also quitted his mortal coil at Varanasi in the year 1626 AD, at the ripe old age of 126 years. Though his body perished, his fame still survives.

8

Places And Spots Associated With Tulsidas

(i) Kashi: This eternal city of India, now called Varanasi, had been the main place of action for Tulsidas. It still has a ghat named after Tulsidas. In fact, some of the localities like Lanka and Nak-Katiyya are those localities which acquired this name when, at the bidding of Tulsidas, people started staging various activities associated with Ram Leela. Near Durga Temple on Durgakunda Road is also situated the famous 'Tulsidas Manas Mandir'. It is dedicated to the great epic poem 'Sri Ramcharitamanas' written by Tulsidas. It has all the seven cantos engraved on the walls with murals depicting the incidents from the great epic.

(ii) Prayag: Now called Allahabad and renamed as Prayag after the great Kumbha fair of 2001 AD, it has many places associated with Tulsidas. Prominent among them are the 'Akshaya Bat', that 'Immortal Banyan' beneath which Tulsidas met the ancient sages Yagyavakkya and Bharadwaj. Still there is a place called

Bharadwaj Ashram. Tulsidas has vividly described the Magh Mela that still takes place annually in Allahabad.

(iii) Rajapur: It is a small village on the banks of the river Yamuna in the district of Banda. It is generally believed to be Tulsidas' birth place.

(iv) Soron: Also called in mythological accounts the Sookar-Kshetra, it is a small place near Badayun district in UP, on the banks of the river Ganga. It was at this place that Tulsidas heard the 'Ram-Katha' for the first time from his Guru Swami Narharyananda.

(v) Manasarovar: It is a famous lake in Tibet but a revered place for the Hindus. Tulsidas, it is said had visited it. Impressed by its serenity and quietude, he used this place allegorically to call his epic poem "Sriramcharita Manas".

9

Famous Poems, Orisons, Panegyric Poems, Bhajans and Prayers of Tulsidas

गोस्वामी तुलसीदास कृत गणेश-प्रार्थना

('विनय-पत्रिका' से)

मूलः

गाइए गणपति जग-वन्दन
संकर-सुवन, भवानी नंदन
गाइए गणपति जग-वन्दन
सिद्धि सदन गजवदन विनायक
कृपा-सिंधु सुन्दर सब लायक
मोदक प्रिय मुद-मंगल दाता
विद्या-वारिध, बुद्धि विधाता
माँगत तुलसीदास कर जोरे
बसें राम-सिय मानस मोरे!

अर्थः आइए समस्त जगत द्वारा वंदित गणपति के गुणगान करें। वे भगवान शंकर और भवानी (पार्वती) के पुत्र हैं, सिद्धि के धाम और हाथी के चेहरेवाले विनायक हैं। उन्हें लड्डू प्रिय हैं और वे प्रसन्नता और मंगल के दाता हैं, विद्या के सागर और बुद्धि के विधाता हैं-मेरी उनसे हाथ जोड़कर प्रार्थना है कि वह श्रीराम और सीता जी को मेरे मन में बसा दें।

(i) A Prayer to Lord Ganesh
Composed by Goswami Tulsidas
[From 'VINAYA PATRIKA]

Text:

Gaiye Ganapati jag-vandan
Sankar-suvan Bhavāni nandan
Gaiye Ganapati jag-vandan
Siddhi sadan Gaj-vandan Vinayak
Kripa-sindhu sundar sab layak
Modak priya mud-mangal dātā
Vidya-varidhi buddhi vidhātā
Mangat Tulsidas kar jore
Basen Ram-Siya mānas more!

Meaning: Come, let us sing the virtues of Ganapati whom the whole world worships. He is the son of Lord Shankar and Bhavani (Parvati ji); the abode of Siddhi. This elephant-faced Great Leader loves laddoos and he bestows happiness and welfare to all. He is the repository of knowledge and the god of wisdom. I pray him hand-bound to make Lord Ram and Sita ever dwell in my heart.

ध्यान

(तुलसी विरचित)

शान्तं शाश्वतप्रमेयनघं निर्वाण शान्तिप्रदं
ब्रह्मश्अम्भुणीन्द्रसेव्यमनिशं वेदान्त वेद्यं विभुम्।
रामाश्यं जगदीश्वरं सुरगुरं मायामनुष्यं हरिम्।
वन्देहं करुणाकरं रघुवरं भूपाल चूड़ामणिम्।

शान्त, सनातम, प्रमाणों से परे, निष्पाप, निर्वाणरूपी परम शान्ति देने वाले, ब्रह्मा, शंभु और शेष जी से निरन्तर पूजित, वेदान्त के द्वारा उद्घाटित, सर्वव्यापक, देवताओं में सबसे बड़े, अपनी माया से मनुष्य रूप में दिखने वाले, समस्त पापों का हरण करने वाले, करूणा की खान, रघुकुल में श्रेष्ठ तथा समस्त भूपालों (राजाओं) के शिरोमणि, राम कहलाने वाले जगत के ईश्वर रूप की मैं वन्दना करता हूँ।

(ii) Meditation

(By Tulsidas From the 'Manas')

Shantam shashwatamaprameya managham nirvān
shāntipradam

Brahma Shambhu phaneedrasevyamanisham vedant
vedyam vibhum|

Rāmākhyam jagdeeshwaram suragurum maya
manushyam harim

Vandeaham karunakaram Raghuvaram
bhoopalachoodamanim||

Him I adore, the serene, the eternal, beyond all means of cognition, the sinless, who grants the peace of final liberation, whom Brahma, Shambhu and the Serpent King always pay reverence, revealed by Vedanta; all-pervading, Lord of the world, preceptor of thc gods, appearing in human form through his Maya (Illusive creation), the crest-jewel of kings, in whom all mercy dwells, prince of the house of Raghu, who is famous by the name Ram!

एक प्रार्थना
(तुलसीकृत 'श्री रामचरितमानस' से)

नमामि भक्त वत्सलं कृपालु शील कोमलं॥
भजामि ते पदाम्बुजं अकामिना स्वधामदं॥
निकाम श्याम सुंदरं भवाम्बुनाथ मंदरं॥
प्रफुल्ल कंज लोचनं । मदादि दोष मोचनं॥
प्रलम्ब बाहु विक्रमं । प्रभोमेय वैभवं॥
निषंग चाप सायकं । धरं त्रिलोक नायकं॥
दिनेश वंश मंडनं । महेश चाप खंडनं॥
मुनिन्द्र संत रंजनं । सुरारि वृन्द भंजनं॥
मनोज वैरि वंदितं । अजादि देव सेवितं॥
विशुद्ध बोध विग्रहं । समस्त दूषणा पहं॥
नमामि इंदिरा पतिं । सुखाकरं सतां गतिं॥
भजे सशक्ति सानुजं । शची पति प्रियानुजं॥
त्वदंघ्रि मूलं ये नराः । भजंति हीन मत्सराः॥
पतंति नो भवार्ण वे । वितर्क वीचि संकुले॥
विविक्त वासिनः सदा । भजंति मुक्त ये मुदा॥
निरस्य इंद्रियादिकं । प्रपांति ते गतिं स्वकं॥
तमेकमद्भुतं प्रभु निरीहमीश्वरं विभुं।
जगत गुरूं च शाश्वतं । तुरीयमेव केवलं॥
भजामि भाव वल्लभं । कुयोगिनां सुदुर्लभं॥
स्वभक्त कल्प पादपं । समं सुसेव्यमन्वहं॥
अनूप रूप भूपतिं । नतोऽमुर्विजा पतिं॥
प्रसीद मे नमामि ते । पदाब्ज भक्ति देहि मे॥
पठंति ये स्तवं इदं । नरादरेण ते पदं॥
व्रजंति नात्र संशयं । त्वदीय भक्ति संयुताः॥

(iii) A Prayer

(By Tulsidas From the 'Sriramcharita manas')

Namāmi bhakta vatsalam | Kripālu sheela komalam | |
Bhajami te padāmbujam | Akāmina swadhamadam | |
Nikam shyām sundaram | Bhavāmbunath mandaram | |
Prafulla kanja lochanam | Madādi dosh mochanam | |
Pralambu bāhu vikramam | Prabhoaprameya vaibhavam | |
Nishang chap sayakam | Dharam trilok nayakam | |
Dinesh vansha mandanam | Mahesh chap kahandanam | |
Muneendra sant ranjanam | Surāri vrinda bhanjanam | |
Manoj vairi vanditam | Ajādi deva sevitam | |
Vishuddha bodha vigraham | Samasta dooshanā paham | |
Namāmi Indirā patim | Sukhānkram satam gatim | |
Bhaje sashakti sānujam | Shachi Pati priyānujam | |
Twadanghri moola ye narah | Bhajanti heena matsarah | |
Patanti no bhavarna ve | Vitarke veechi samkule | |
Vivakta vasinah sadā | Bhajanti muktaye mudā | |
Nirasya indriyadikam | Prapanti te gatim swakam | |
Tameka madbhutam prabhum | Nireehameeshwaram vibhum | |
Jagat-gurum cha shashwatam | Tureeyameva kevalam | |
Bhajāmi bhāv vallabham | Kuyogina sudurlabham | |
Swabhakta kalpa padapam | Samam susevyamanvaham | |
Anoop roop bhoopatim | Natoahmurvija patim | |
Praseeda me namāmi te | Padabja bhakti dehi me | |
Pathāni ye stvavam idam | Naradarena te padam | |
Vrajanti natra samshayam | Twadeeya bhakti samyutah | |

हे भक्तवत्सल! हे कृपालु! हे कोमल स्वभाव वाले! मैं आपको नमस्कार करता हूँ। निष्काम जनों को अपना परमधाम देने वाले आपके चरण कमलों को मैं भेजता हूँ। आप सुन्दर, श्याम, संसार रूपी समुद्र को मथने के लिए मंदराचल हैं। आप फूले हुए कमल के समान नेत्रों वाले और मदादि दोषों से मुक्ति दिलाने वाले हैं। हे प्रभो! आपकी लम्बी भुजाओं का पराक्रम और आपका ऐश्वर्य असीम है। हे तरकश और धनुषबाण धारण करने वाले तीनों लोकों के स्वामी! सूर्य वंश के भूषण, महादेव जी के धनुष को तोड़ने वाले, मुनिराजों और संतों को आनन्द देने वाले देवताओं के शत्रु असुरों के समूहों का नाश करने वाले हैं। आप कामदेव के शत्रु महादेव जी द्वारा वन्दित, ब्रह्मादि देवताओं द्वारा सेवित विशुद्ध ज्ञानमय विग्रह और सभी दोषों को नष्ट करने वाले हैं। हे लक्ष्मी पते[1] । हे सुखों की खान और सत्पुरुषों की एकमात्र गति (या गंतव्य) मैं आपको नमस्कार करताा हूँ।

हे शची पति(इन्द्र) के छोटे भाई[2] मैं आपको आपकी स्वशक्ति श्री सीता जी सहित और छोटे भाई लक्ष्मण सहित नमन (भजन) करता हूँ। जो मनुष्य डाह रहित होकर आपके चरणकमलों का सेवन (पूजन) करते है वे तर्क-वितर्क रूपी तरंगों से भरे संसार रूपी समुद्र में नहीं गिरते। जो एकांत वासी पुरुष मुक्ति के लिए इन्द्रियादि का निग्रह करके प्रसन्न होकर आपका भजन करते हैं, वे अपने (सही रूप से अर्जित) स्वरूप को प्राप्त होते हैं। उनको-(आपको) जो एक अद्‌भुत, प्रभु (सर्व समर्थ) इच्छा रहित ईश्वर, व्यापक, जगद्‌गुरु, सनातन (नित्य) तुरीय (इन्द्रियातीत या तीनों लोकों से परे) और केवल (अपने) स्वरूप में स्थित हैं, जो भावना प्रिय, कुयोगियों दुष्टों के लिए अत्यंत दुर्लभ और अपने भक्तों के लिए कल्पवृक्ष सम पक्षपात रहित और सदा सुखपूर्वक सेवन करने के योग्य हैं- मैं निरंतर भजता हूँ। हे अनुपम सुन्दर! हे पृथ्वीपति! हे जानकीनाथ! मैं आपको प्रणाम करता हूँ। मुझ पर प्रसन्न होइए। मुझे (सदैव) अपने चरण कमलों के प्रति भक्ति दीजिए। जो मनुष्य इस स्तुति को आदर पूर्वक पढ़ते हैं वे भक्ति से युत होकर आपके परम पद को प्राप्त होते हैं (अर्थात् आपके लोक में स्थायी निवास पाते हैं) इसमे कोई संदेह नहीं ।

---

१ चूँकि राम विष्णु के अवतार थे और विष्णु लक्ष्मी के पति इसलिए ऐसा सम्बोधन प्रयुक्त किया गया है।
२ विष्णु इन्द्र के छोटे भाई थे। दोनों के माता-पिता कश्यप और अदिति थे।

I reverence you, who his faithful devotees, and is gracious and kind hearted. I adore your lotus feet which vouchsafe to your selfless lover a place in your own abode. I worship you, O Lord, having exquisitely beautiful swarthy form; the mount Mandar to churn the ocean of physical existence; whose eyes are like the full blown lotus. You are the saviour from arrogance and every other sin. Immense is the might of your long arms and immeasurable is your wealth. You carry on your person a quiver and an arrow, O Ruler of the three worlds! You are an ornament of the Solar race, the breaker of Mahesh's (Shiv's) bow, joy of high saints and sages, destroyer of the demon hosts. You are worshipped by Kama's foe (Shiv) and reverenced by Brahma and all the gods. You who are an embodiment of purest wisdom, destroyer of all vices, I adore you, O Lakshmi's Lord[1], mine of bliss and salvation of the holy!

I worship you, your consort and your brother; you are the beloved younger brother of Shachi's lord[2]. Men who unenviously worship your lotus feet fall not into the ocean of physical existence, turbulent with the billows of wrangling. The solitaires who ever worship you in the glad hope of liberation, with every sensual sense subdued, attain to that salvation which is deservedly their own.

You I adore, the mysterious Lord, the passion less and all pervading sovereign, the eternal guru of the world, the perfect mystic. One alone, lover of love, transcending the three Gunas (the three fundamental properties of the existence: Satva, Rajas and Tamas) and all absolute (self-existent). I adore you, who is fond of devotion, who is most difficult to access to sensual strivers, but a Tree of Paradise to his own worshippers, impartial and ever worthy to be worshipped.

To you I do obeisance, sovereign of matchless beauty, Lord of the earth-born (Sita). I reverence you, be gracious unto me and grant me devotion to your feet.

Men who recite this hymn with reverence indoubtably attain your abode, acquiring devotion to your feet simultaneously.

---

1. Ram was Incarnation of Lord Vishnu, the Lord of Lakshmi.

2. Since Vishnu was the younger brother of Indra, the spouse of Shachi, Ram is also addressed in the same relationship as he was Vishnu's Incarnated form.

एक स्तवक
(तुलसीकृत 'रामचरित मानस' से)

जय राम रमारमनं समनं।
भव ताप भयाकुल पाहिजनं॥
अवधेस सुरेस रमेस विभो।
सरनागत माँगत पाहि प्रभो॥। ॥

हे राम! हे रमा-रमण (रमा अर्थात् लक्ष्मी के साथ विहार करने वाले)! हे जन्म-मरण के दुख को नष्ट करने वाले। आपकी जय हो। आवागमन के भय से व्याकुल इस सेवक की रक्षा कीजिए। हे अवधपति! हे देवताओं के स्वामी। हे रमापति। हे विभो! मैं शरणागत आपसे यही मांगता हूँ कि हे प्रभु! मेरी रक्षा कीजिए॥। ॥

दससीस विनासन बीस भुजा।
कृति दूरि महा महिभूरि रुजा॥
रजनीचर वृन्द पतंग रहे।
सर पावक तेज प्रचंड दहे॥२॥

हे दस सिर और बीस भुजाओं वाले रावण का विनाश कर के मही (पृथ्वी) के सब कष्टों को दूर करने वाले श्रीराम राक्षस समूह रूपी जो पतंगे थे वे सब (आपके) बाण रूपी अग्नि के प्रचण्ड तेज से जल गए॥२॥

महि मंडल मंडन चारुतरं।
धृत सायक चाप निषंग बरं॥
मद मोह महा ममता रजनी।
तम पुंज दिवाकर तेज अनी॥३॥

(iv) A Panegyric Poem

(By Tulsidas's 'Sri Ramcharita manas')

Jai Rām Ramā ramanam samanam
Bhava tāp bhayakul pathi janam|
Avadhesa suresa Ramesh vibho
Saranāgat mangat pahi prabho ||1||

Glory to Ram, Sita's (or Lakshman's) lord, subduer of the pains of mundane existence! Protect your servants as all are unnerved by the dread of transmigration! O King of Avadh, Lord of Heaven, Lakshmi's spouse, sovereign Lord! I come to thee for refuge, Lord, and crave protection. ||1||

Dasaseesa vināshan bees bhuja
Krita doorimaha mahi bhoori ruja|
Rajaneechar vrinda patang rahe
Sar pāvak tej prachanda dahe ||2||

You did slay the demon with ten heads and twenty arms and rid the earth of many a severe scourge. The host of demons were a veritable sworn of moth-flies that were reduced to ashes by the fierce flame of your fiery arrows. ||2||

Mahi mandal mandan chāru taram
Dhrita sayak chāp nishang baram|
Mada moha mahā mamtā rajani
Tam punja diwākar tej anee||3||

श्रेष्ठ बाण, धनुष और तूणीर धारणा किए, हे श्रीराम! आपके पृथ्वी मंडल के श्रेष्ठतम आभूषण हैं। अधिक मद, मोह और ममतारूपी रात्रि के अंधकार सूमह को नष्ट करने के लिए सूर्य के तेजोमय किरणों के समूह हैं॥३॥

मन जात किरात निपात किए।
मृग लोग कुभोग सरेन हिए॥
हति नाथ अनाथनि पाहि हरे।
विषया बन पाँवर भूलि परे॥४॥

कामदेव रूपी भील ने मनुष्य रूपी हिरनों के हृदय में कुभोग रूपी बाण मारकर उन्हें गिरा दिया। हे नाथ! हे हरे! उसे मार का विषय रूपी वन में भूले पड़े इन पामर अनाथ जीवों की रक्षा कीजिए॥४॥

बहु रोग वियोगगन्हि लोग हुए।
भवदंघ्रि निरादर के फल ए॥
भव सिंधु अगाध परे नर ते।
पद पंकज प्रेम न जे करते॥५॥

बहुत से लोग रोगों और वियोगों के मारे हुए हैं-ये आपके चरणों का आदर न करने का फल है। जो मनुष्य आपके चरण कमलों से प्रेम नहीं करते, वे ही अथाह भवसागर में जाके पड़ते हैं। ॥५॥

अति दीन मलीन दुखी नित हौं।
जिनके पद पंकज प्रीति नहीं॥
अवलम्ब भवंत कथा जिनके।
प्रिय संत अनन्त सदा तिनके॥६॥

जिनको आपके कमलों से स्नेह नहीं, वे नित्य ही अत्यन्त दीन, मलिन और दुखी रहते हैं। जिनको अपकी लीला-कथा का सहारा है उनको संत और भगवान सदा प्रिय लगते हैं॥६॥

Most lovely ornament of the terrestial globe, bearing the beauteous bow, arrows and quiver, you quelled the arrogance and folly and profound infatuation to self as the blazing rays of the sun scatter the deep darkness of night. ||3||

Man jāt kirāt nipāt kiye
Mriga log kubhog saren hiye|
Hati nāth anāthani pahi hare
Vishaya ban pānwar bhooli pare ||4||

As a Kirat (bheela) pierces a deer with his arrow, so has Kamdeva vanquished the hearts of men with the weapon of sensual desire. Strike him, Lord Hari and save thy wretched creatures, masterless and lost in the forest of carnal lust. ||4||

Bahu rog viyoganhi log haye
Bhava danghrih niradar ke phal ye|
Bhav sindhu agādh pare nar te
Pad pankaj prem na je karate ||5||

Men have been afflicted with numberless diseases, pains of bereavement and all these result out of the contempt shown for your feet. Verily those who have no love for your lotus feet have fallen into the bottomless ocean of morality. ||5||

Ati deen maleen dukhee nita heen
Jinken pad-pankaj preeti naheen|
Avalamb bhavanta katha jinken
Priya santa ananta sada tinken ||6||

They are most wretched, impure and unhappy who have no devotion to your lotus feet. But who make your tale of glory their support, ever hold dear those who are constant in their noble observance. ||6||

नहिं राग न लोभ न मान सदा।
तिन्ह के सम वैभव वा विपदा।।
ऐहि ते सब सेवक होत मुदा।
मुनि त्यागत जोग भरोस सदा।।७।।

उनमें न आसक्ति है न लोभ, न मान और न मद। उनके लिए संपत्ति और विपत्ति समान हैं। इसीलिए मुनि लोग योग का भरोसा भी सदा के लिए त्याग प्रसन्नता से आपके सेवक बन जाते हैं।।७।।

करि प्रेम निरंतर नेम लिएँ।
पदपंकज सेवत सुद्ध हिएँ।।
सम मानि निरादर आदर ही।
सब संत सुखी विचरंति मही।।८।।

वे प्रेमपूर्वक नियम से और शुद्ध हृदय से आपके चरणों की सेवा करते रहते हैं और आदर-निरादर को समान मान कर वे संत सुखपूर्वक इस पृथ्वी पर विचरण करते रहते हैं।।८।।

मुनि-मानस पंकज-भृंग भजे।
रघुवीर महा रनधीर अजे।।
तव नाम जपामि नमामि हरी।
भव रोग महागद मान अरी।।९।।

हे मुनियों के मन रूपी कमल के भ्रमर! हे महा रणधीर एवम् अजेय श्री रघुवीर! मैं आपका भजन करता हूँ। हे हरि! आपका नाम जपता हूँ और आपको नमस्कार करता हूँ। आपके भवसागर रूपी रोग की महान औषधि हैं और अभिमान के शत्रु हैं।।९।।

गुण शील कृपा परमायतनं।
प्रनमामि निरंतर श्री रमनं।।
रघुनन्द निकंदय द्वंद्वघनं।।
महिपाल विलोकय दीनजनं।।१०।।

आप गुण, शील और कृपा के परम स्थान हैं। आप लक्ष्मीपति हैं। मैं आपको निरंतर प्रणाम करता हूँ। हे रघुनन्दन! द्वन्द्व समूह को नष्ट कीजिए। हे पृथ्वी का पालन करने वाले राजन्! इस दीन जन की ओर भी देखिए।।१०।।

Nahin rāg na lobha nā mān sadā
Tinhke sam vaibhav va vipadā|
Ehi te sab sewak hota mudā
Muni tyagat jog bharosa sadā ||7||

They are free from passion, greed, pride and arrogance; prosperity and adversity are alike to them. That is why sages ever abandon reliance on ascetic practice and gladly become your servants. ||7||

Kari prem nirantar nem liyen
Pad-pankah sewit siddha hiyen|
Sam māni nirādar ādar hee
Sab santa sukhee vicharanti mahee ||8||

They wait upon your lotus feet devoutly and unceasingly with a pure heart and with strict observance. Regarding contempt and respect as one, saints all wander happily about the earth. ||8||

Muni-mānas pankaj-bhringa bhaje
Raghuveer mahā ranadheer aje|
Tav nām japami namāmi haree
Bhava rog mahāgad mān aree ||9||

O you, who haunt the souls of sages as a bee the lotus! O Raghuveer, mighty and unconquerable hero! I worship thee! The name I repeat, O Hari, and adore thee, the potent remedy for the sickness of morality and foe of pride. ||9||

Guna sheela kreepā paramāyatanam
Pranamāmi nirantar shree ramanam |
Raghunanda nikandaya dwanḍa ghanam
Mahipāl vilokaya deen janam ||10||

O ultimate repository of goodness, loving kindness and grace, I bow unceasingly before thee, O Lakshmi's Lord! O Delight of the Raghus, destroy the pairs of contraiety! Sovereign of earth, look graciously upon thy lowly servant. ||10||

एक स्तुति
(तुलसीकृत'श्री रामचरितमानस से')

जय सगुन निर्गुन रूप रूप अनूप भूप सिरोमने।
दसकंधरादि प्रचंड निसिचर प्रबल खल भुजबल हने।।
अवतार नर संसार भार विभंजि दारून दुख दहे।
जय प्रनतपाल दयाल प्रभु संजुक्त सक्ति नमामहे।।१।।

हे सगुन और निर्गुन रूप! हे अनुपम लावण्ययुक्त! हे राजाओं के शिरोमणि! आपकी जय हो! आपने रावणादि प्रचण्ड, प्रबल और दुष्ट राक्षसों को अपनी भुजाओं के बल से मार डाला। आपने नर रूप में अवतार लेकर संसार के भार को नष्ट करके अत्यन्त कठोर दुखों का दहन कर दिया। हे दयालु! हे शरण में आए हुए की रक्षा करने वाले प्रभो! आपकी जय हो। मैं शक्ति (सीता) सहित आप शक्तिमान को नमस्कार करता हूँ।।!।।

तव विषम माया बस सुरासर नाग नर अग जग हरे।
भव पंथ भ्रमित अमित दिवस निसि काल कर्मगुननि भरे।।
जो नाथ करि करुना बिलोके त्रिविध दुख ते निर्बहे।
भव खेद छेदन दच्छ हम कहँ रच्छ राम नमामहे।।२।।

हे हरे! आपकी विषय माया के वशीभूत होने के कारण देवता, राक्षंस, नाग, नर और चर-अचर, सभी काल, कर्म और गुणों से भरे हुए दिन-रात भव सागर में भटक रहे हैं। हे नाथ! इनमें जिनको आपने कृपा दृष्टि से देख लिया, वे तीनों प्रकार के दुखों से छूट गए। हे आवागमन के श्रम (परेशानी) को दूर करने में समर्थ श्री राम! हमारी रक्षा कीजिए। हम आपको नमस्कार करते हैं।।२।।

(v) An Orison
(From Tulsidas's Sriramcharita manas)

Jai saguna nirguna roop roop anoop bhoop siromane |
Daskandharādi prachanda nisachar prabal khal bhujabal hane ||
Avatār nar sansār bhār vibhanji daruna dukh dahe |
Jai pranatapal dayāl prabhu samjukta sakti namāmahe ||1||

Glory to the crest-jewel of kings, of incomparable beauty; O personal and impersonal form of Lord Almighty! You have slain Ravan and all the other formidable, powerful and evil demons. Glory to thee! Descending in the form of man, you have rid the world of its burden and burnt to ashes its tormenting woes! Glory to thee, the merciful Lord, protector of the supplicant. Thee we adore together with thy consort, the. power of the powerful. ||1||

Tav visham māyā bas sursur nāg nar aga jag harc |
Bhav pantha bhramita amita diwas nisi kal karam gunani bhare ||
Jo nath kari karuna biloke trividha dukha te nirbahe ||
Bhav kheda chhedan daccha ham kahn raccha Ram namāmahe ||2||

Subject to your inescapable Maya (the power of illusive creation), O Hari, are the gods and demons, serpents and human beings and all creations animate or inanimate, a prey to fate and destiny and nature's basic elements; but they on whom you look, O Lord, with a eye on compassion have been delivered from all the three kinds of afflictions. Save us, O you, who knows well how to banish the toils metempsychosis! O Ram we adore thee! ||2||

जे ग्यान मान विमत्त तव भव हरनि भक्ति न आदरी।
ते पाइ सुर दुर्लभ पदादपि परत हम देखत हरी।।
बिस्वास करि सब आस परिहरि दास तव जे होइ रहे।
जपि नाम तव बिनु श्रम तरहिं भव नाथ सो समरामहे।।३।।

जिन्होंने मिथ्याज्ञान के अभिमान मे मतवाले होकर जन्म मृत्यु को हरने वाली आपकी भक्ति का आदर नहीं किया, हे हरि! उन्हें देव-दुर्लभ पद को पाकर भी हम उस पद से नीचे गिरते देखते हैं। जो सब आशाओं को त्याग कर केवल आप पर विश्वास कर आपके दास हो जाते हैं, वे केवल आपका नाम ही जप कर बिना मेहनत के संसार रूपी सागर से पार हो जाते हैं। हे नाथ! इस प्रकार हम आपका स्मरण करते हैं। ।।३।।

जो चरन सिव अज पूज्य रज सुभ परसि मुनि पतिनी तरी।
नख निर्गता मुनि वंदिता त्रैलोक्य पावनि सुरसरी।।
ध्वज कुलिस अंकुस कज जुत बन फिरत कंटक किन लहे।
पद कंज द्वंद्व मुकुंद राम रमेस नित्य भजामहे।।४।।

जो चरण शिवजी और ब्रह्माजी द्वारा पूज्य हैं तथा जिन चरणों की कल्याणमयी रज का स्पर्श पाकर गौतम ऋषि की पत्नी (अहिल्या) तर गई, जिन चरणों के नख से मुनियों द्वारा वंदित, तीनों लोकों को पवित्र करने वाली देव नदी गंगाजी निकली और जो ध्वजा, वज्र, अंकुश और कमल-इन चिन्हों से युक्त हैं तथा जिन के चरणों में वन में घूमते समय काँटे चुभ जाने से निशान पड़ गए हैं, हे मुकुन्द[1] ! हे राम! हे रमापति! हम आपके उन्हीं दोनों चरण-कमलों का नित्य भजन करते रहते हैं।।४।।

---

1. मोक्ष देने वाला ।

Je gyān mān vimatta tav bhav harani bhakti ne ādaree |
Te pai sur durlabh padādapi parat ham dekhat haree ||
Biswās kari sab āsa parihari dās tav je hoi rahe |
Japi nām tav binu sram tarahin bhav nath so samaramahe ||3||

When men, intoxicated with the pride of wisdom, despise their faith in you which frees one from the bonds of rebirth, even though they reach that goal, O Hari, which gods may scarcely reach, we see them falling from that high status. But those who place their trust in you, abandoning all other hope, become and remain your servants; ever repeating your, O Lord, in prayer, they cross without efforts sea of mundane existence-therefore, O Master we remember only thee. ||3||

Je charan Siva Aja poojya raja subha parasi muni patini taree |
Nakh nirgatā muni vanditā trailokya pāvani surasaree ||
Dhwaja kulis ankusa kanja juta ban phirat kantak kin lahe |
Pada kanj dwandwa mukunda Ram ramesh nitya namāmahe ||4||

Those feet which Shiv and Brahma reverence, those feet by the touch of whose blessed dust the sage's wife (Ahilya) was redeemed; those feet from whose nails sprang forth the sacred river which is ever reverenced by sages and which purifies the three spheres; those feet that bear the mark of the flag, the thunderbolt, the goad and the lotus, which were pierced by thorns as they wandered in the woods, even those two lotus feet, Mukunda[1], Ram, Sita's lord we ever worship. ||4||

1. Granter of salvation or the final release.

अव्यक्तमूलमनादि तरु त्वच चारि निगमागम भने।
षट कंध साखा पंच बीस अनेक पर्न सुमन घने॥
फल जुगल विधि कटु मधुर बेलि अकेलि जेहि आश्रित रहे।
पल्लवित फूलत नवल नित संसार विटप नमामहे॥५॥

वेद -शास्त्रों ने कहा है कि जिसका मूल अव्यक्त है, जो अनादि है, जिसके चार त्वचाएँ, छह तने, पच्चीस शाखाएँ और अनेकों पत्ते और बहुत से फूल हैं, जिसमे कड़वे और मीठे दो प्रकार के फल लगे हैं, जिस पर एक ही बेल हैं, जो उसी के आश्रय पर रहती है, जिसमे नित नए पत्ते और फूल निकलते रहते हैं ऐसे विश्व रूप में प्रकट आपको हम नमस्कार करते हैं[1] ॥५॥

---

1. 'चेतना की चार अवस्थाएँ है। जागृति, स्वप्न, सुषुप्ति और तुरीयावस्था, जो यहाँ तने की चार त्वचाएँ कही गई है। अस्तित्व की हर अवस्थाएँ: होना, प्रकट होना, परिवर्तित होना, क्षयग्रसित होना और विलीन हो जाना यहाँ छह तने कहे गए हैं। पच्चीस शाखाएँ हैं वह जिससे यह मर्त्य लोक बना है प्रकृति महत् अंकहार, मानस चित्त तथा पाँच तन्मात्रा (सूक्ष्म तत्त्व) पाँच महाभूत (पंच तत्त्व) तथा पाँच ज्ञानेन्दिय। लता यहाँ सबको ढँकने वाली माया को कहा गया है । यह पूरा रूपक विशुद्ध रूप से उपनिषदों का निचोड़ है। और पेड़ का यह रूपक सनातम धर्म के विचारकों को बड़ा प्रिय अवलम्बन है जो समग्र सृष्टि के अस्तित्व को रूपायित करता है।

Avyaktamoolamanādi taru twacha chari nigamāgam bhane |
Shata kandha sākhā pancha beesa aneka parna suman ghane ||
Phal jugal vidha katu madhur beli akeli jehi ashrita rahe |
Pallavita phoolat naval nita sansara vitapa namāmahe ||5||

We adore the tree of manifest world, Vedas and scriptures have declared it to be without origin and its roots unmanifest. Its coats of bark are four; its stems are six; its branches are twenty five; countless leaves, many the flowers it bears; it puts forth two kinds of fruit; one sour, one sweet; there is only one creeper that clings there to, and ever bears fresh fruits and blossoms[1]. ||5||

---

1. The four states of consciousness viz., life, dream, sound sleep and the pure impersonal state (tkx`fr] LoIu] lq"kqfIr and rqjh;) are the four coats of bark; six states of existence are (i) to be (ii) to come into being (iii) to undergo transformation (iv) to grow (v) to decay, (vi) to perish which are the six stems referred to here. The twenty five branches of this tree are the categories this plenum is composed of. They are Prakrati or Primodial Matter, Mahat or Cosmic Reason; Akankar or cosmic ego-sense; Manas or the cosmic mind; chitta or the cosmic intellect; plus five senses of perception, five 'tan-matra' or subtle elements, the five Mahabhoot or five basic elements plus five senses of wisdom (KkusfUnz;). The creeper referred to is Maya.

जे ब्रह्म अजमद्वैतमनुभवगम्य मन पर ध्यावहीं।
ते कहहूँ जानहुँ नाथ हम तव सगुन जस तिन गावहीं।
करुनायतन प्रभु सदगुनाकर देव यह वर माँगहीं।
मन वचन कर्म विकार तजि तव चरण। हम अनुरागहीं।।६।।

ब्रह्म अजन्मा है, अद्वैत है, अनुभव से ही जाना जाता है और जो मन से परे है- जो ब्रह्म का ध्यान करते हैं वे ऐसा कहा करें और जाना करें, हे नाथ! हम तो आपका नित्य सुगण यश ही गाते है। हे करूणा के धाम प्रभु! हे सद्‌गुणों की खान! हे देव! यह वरदान माँगते हैं कि मन, वचन और कर्म से विकारों को त्याग कर हम सदा आपके चरणों में ही प्रेम करें।।६।।

Je Brahma Ajamadwaitamanubhavagamaya man par dhyāvaheen |
Te kāhahun janahun Nath ham tava saguna jas nita gavaheen ||
Karunayatan Prabhu sadgunākar Dev yaha bara māngaheen |
Man vachan karma vikar taji tava charan ham anurāgaheen ||6||

Let those who contemplate the absulete, ever lasting and without a second, attainable by self-realisation, beyond intellectual reach, speak of 'It' and know 'It', we, O Lord, hymn unceasingly the glory as personal! O home of compassion, Lord, in whom all goodness dwells, divine being; this is the boon we crave; that casting off all aberration of all thought, word and deed, we may be only devoted to your feet. ||6||

एक प्रार्थना
(तुलसीकृत'श्री रामचरित मानस से')

मामभिरक्षय रघुकुलनायक। धृत बर चाप रुचिर कर सायक।।
मोह महा घन पटल प्रभंजन । संसय विपिन अनल सुर रंजन।।
अगुन सगुन गुन मंदिर सुंदर। भ्रमतम प्रबल प्रताप दिवाकर।।
काम क्रोध मद गज पंचानन। बसहु निरंतर जन मन कानन।।
विषय मनोरथ पुंज कंज बन। प्रबल तुषार उदास पार मन।।
भव बारिधि मंदर परमंदर। बारद तारय संसृति दुस्तर।।
स्याम गात राजीव विलोचन। दीन बन्धु प्रन तारति मोचन।।
अनुज जानकी सहित निरंतर । बसहु राम नृप मम उर अंतर।
मुनि रंजन महि मंडल मंडन। तुलसीदास प्रभु त्रास बिखंडन।

(vi) A Prayer
(From Tulsidas's Sriramcharita manas)

Mamabhi rakshyaya Raghukul nāyak |
Dhrita bar chap ruchir kar sāyak ||
Moha mahā ghan patal prabhanjan |
Sansaya vipin anal sura ranjan ||
Aguna saguna guna mandir sundar |
Bhrama tama prabal pratap diwākar ||
Kama krodha mada gaj panchānan |
.Sabahu nirantar jan man kānan ||
Vishaya manorath punj kanja bana |
Prabal tushār udār pār mana ||
Bhava baridha mandar parmandar |
Barad tāraya sansrita dustar ||
Syam gata rajeeva vilochana |
Deenabandhu prana tārati mochan ||
Anuj Jānakee sahita nirantar |
Basahu Rām nripa mam ur antar ||
Muni ranjan mahi mandal mandan |
Tulsidās prabhu trās bikhandan ||

हे रघुकुल नायक। सुन्दर हाथों में श्रेष्ठ और सुन्दर बाण धारण किए हुए, आप मेरी रक्षा कीजिए। आप महामोहरूपी मेघ-समूह के लिए प्रचण्ड पवन हैं, संशय रूपी वन के लिए अग्नि हैं और देवताओं को आनन्द देने वाले हैं। आप निर्गुण, सगुण दिव्यगुणों के धाम और परम सुन्दर हैं। भ्रम रूपी अंधकार के लिए प्रबल प्रतापी सूर्य हैं। काम, क्रोध और मदरूपी हाथियों के लिए सिंह के समान आप इस सेवक के मनपी रूपी वन में निरंतर वास कीजिए। आप उदार हैं और मन से परे (इन्द्रियातीत) हैं। भवसागर के लिए आप मंदराचल पर्वत (के समान दृढ़) हैं। आप हमारे मन में व्याप्त परम भय को दूर कीजिए और हमें दुस्तर संसार-सागर से पार करवा दीजिए। हे श्याम-सुंदर शरीर और कमल के समान नेत्रों वाले, दीनबंधु! हे शरण में आए हुए दुःख से तुरन्त छुटकारा दिलानेवाले ! हे राजा रामचन्द्र जी! आप छोटे भाई लक्ष्मण और जानकी सहित हमेशा मेरे अन्दर निवास कीजिए। आप मुनियों को आनन्द देने वाले, पृथ्वी मंडल के भूषण, तुलसीदास के प्रभु और भय को नष्ट करने वाले हैं।

O Lord of the house of Raghu who bears in his hand the glorious bow and fine arrows, protect me! O mighty wind to scatter the dence clouds of ignorance, O fire to consume the thicket of doubt, delight of gods, impersonal, personal, fair temple of all perfections, sun to disperse darkness of tolly by the might of your dazzling rays, lion to slay the elephants of lust and wrath and arrogance, dwell ever in the grove which is your servant's heart. Hard frost to wither up the lotus bed of sensual desires, you are generous beyond conception. O Mount Mandara to churn the sea of mundane bonds, deliver me from that which I most dread and bring me safely over the ocean of morality, so hard to cross. O Ram, the king, succour of the meek, reliever of the supplicant's agony, take up your adobe forever in my heart a long with your younger brother and Janaki, O delight of sages, adorement of the earth like a hallow round it, O Lord of Tulsidas, destroyer of the dread!

श्री राम-नाम महिमा

(तुलसीकृत 'रामचरितमानस से')

बंदउँ राम नाम रघुवर को।
हेतु कृसान भानु हिमकर को।।
विधि हरि हरमय वेद प्रान सो।
अगुन अनूपम गुन निधान सो।।१।।

मैं श्री रामचन्द्र जी के नाम 'राम' की वन्दना करता हूँ जो कृशानु, भानु और हिमकर का हेतु है। वह नाम 'राम' ब्रह्मा, विष्णु और शिव रूप है। वह वेदों का प्राण है; निर्गुण अनुपम और गुणों का भंडार है। ।।१।।

महामंत्र जोइ जपत महेसू।
कासी मुकुति हेतु उपदेसू।।
महिमा जासु जान गनराऊ।
प्रथम पूजियत नाम प्रभाऊ।।२।।

वह महामंत्र है जिसका जप शिवजी करते हैं और वही काशी में मुक्ति का कारण बताया गया है; जिसकी महिमा गणेश जी भी जानते हैं। जिनकी इस राम नाम के प्रभाव से ही सबसे पहले पूजा की जाती है ।।२।।

(vii) The Glory of Lord Ram's Name (From Tulsidas's "RAMCHARITA MANAS")

Bandahun Rām nām Raghuvar ko |
Hetu krisān bhānu hinkar ko ||
Vidhi hari haramaya Veda prān so |
Aguna anoopam guna nidhān so ||1||

I salute to the name 'Ram' of the chief of Raghus which is composed of seed letters representing the fire-god, the sun god and the moon-god (viz. 'Ra' 'a' 'm'). It is same as Brahma, Shiva and the vital breath of vedas. It is unqualified, peerless and a mine of all virtues. ||1||

Mahāmantra joi japat Mahesoo |
Kāsi mukuti hetu upadesoo ||
Mahima jāsu jan Ganaraoo |
Prathem poojiyat nām prabhavoo ||2||

It is the great 'Mantra' (holy incantation) which Lord Shiv chants which makes him ensure liberation of the soul at Kashi, Lord Ganesh knows its glory and gets worshipped first of all owing to its influence. ||2||

हरषे हेतु हेरि हर ही को।
किय भूषन तिय भूषन जी को॥
नाम प्रभाउ जान शिव नीको।
कालकूट फल दीन्ह अमी को॥३॥

राम नाम के प्रति पार्वती के हृदय में ऐसी प्रीति देखकर महादेव जी प्रसन्न हो गए और उन्होंने स्त्रियों में भूषण रूप पार्वती को अपना भूषण बना लिया। श्री शिव जी नाम के प्रभाव को भलीभाँति जानते हैं, जिसके कारण कालकूट विष भी उनको अमृत-सा फल देने वाला हो गया ॥३॥

बरषा रितु रघुपति भगति, तुलसी सालि सुदास।
राम नाम बर बरन जुग सावन भादव मास॥

श्री रामचन्द्र जी की भक्ति वर्षा-ऋतु है। तुलसीदास जी कहते हैं कि उत्तम सेवकगण धान हैं और राम नाम के दो सुन्दर अक्षर सावन भादों के दो युगल महीने हैं ॥४॥

आखर मधुर मनोहर दोऊ।
बरन बिलोचन जन जिय जोऊ॥
सुमिरत सुलभ सुखद सब काहू।
लोक लाहु परलोक निबाहू॥५॥

राम नाम के दोनों अक्षर मधुर और मनोहर हैं, वर्णमाला रूपी देह के लोचन हैं, भक्तों के लिए जीवन हैं तथा स्मरण करने पर सबको सुलभ और सुख देने वाले हैं और ये ही इस लोक में लाभ और परलोक में निर्वाह कर्ता हैं। ॥५॥

Harshe hetu heri har hee ko |
Kiya bhooshan tiya bhooshan jee ko ||
Nām prabhau jān Shiv neeko |
Kalkoota phal deeha amee ko ||3||

Discerning the great love for this name in Parvati's heart, Shiv was delighted and let the crown jewel of women become an ornament of his own self. For Shiv had realised the effect of this great name which made the most deadly poison give nectarous effect to his body. ||3||

Barasā ritu Raghupati bhagati Tulsi sāli sudas |
Rām-Nām bara baran jug sāvan bhadava mās ||4||

Devotion to Lord of Raghus is, as it were, the rainy season and the noble devotees, says Tulsidas, represent the paddy crop; while the two charming syllables of the name (Ra-m) stand for the two months - the twins 'Savan' and 'Bhadon' (The most rainy months). ||4||

Akhar mādhur manohar douoo |
Baran bilochan jana jiya jouoo ||
Sumirat sulabha sukhad sab kāhoo |
Lok lahu parlok nibāhoo ||5||

Both the letter sounds are sweet and attractive; they are two eyes, as it were, of the Alphabets (of Nagari script) and the very life of the devotees. Easy to remember and delightful to all, they bring gain here (in this world) and sustenance hereafter. ||5||

कहत सुनत सुमिरत सुठि नीके।
राम लखन सम प्रिय तुलसी के।।
बरनत बरन प्रीति बिलगाती।
ब्रह्मा जीव सम सहत सँघाती।।६।।

ये कहने सुनने और स्मरण करने में बहुत ही सुन्दर और मधुर है और तुलसीदास को तो श्री राम-लक्ष्मण के समान प्रिय हैं इनका अलग-अलग वर्णन करने में प्रीति बिलगाती हैं परन्तु यह जीव और ब्रह्मा के समान स्वभाव से ही साथ रहने वाले हैं।।६।।

नर-नारायण सरिस सुभ्राता।
जग पालक विसेसि जन व्राता।।
भगति सुतिय कल करन विभूषन।
जग हित हेतु विमल विधु पूषन।।७।।

यह दोनों अक्षर नर-नारायण के समान सुन्दर भाई हैं। ये संसार के पालनहार और विशेष रूप से भक्तों की रक्षा करने वाले हैं। ये भक्ति रूपिणी सुन्दर नारी के कानों के आभूषण हैं और जगत के कल्याण के लिए विमल चन्द्रमा और सूर्य हैं।।७।।

स्वाद तोष सम सुगति सुधा के।
कमठ शेष सम धर वसुधा के।।
जनमन मंजु कंज मधुकर के।
जीह जसोमति हरि हलधर के।।८।।

ये मोक्ष रूपी अमृत के स्वाद और तृप्ति के समान है, कच्छप और शेष जी के समान पृथ्वी को धारण करने वाले हैं। ये भक्तों के मनरूपी कमल में विहार करने वाले भ्रमर के समान हैं और जीभ रूपी यशोदा के लिए श्रीकृष्ण और बलराम के समान हैं। ।।८।।

Kaha sunat sumirat suthi neeke |
Ram Lakhan sam priya Tulsee ke ||
Baranat varan preeti bilagātee |
Brahma-jeeva sam sahaj sanghātee ||6||

They are most delightful to utter, hear and remember, and are dear as Ram and Lakshmana to Tulsidas. When treated separately, the two letters lose their harmony whereas they are naturally allied as Brahma (the cosmic spirit) and Jeeva (the individual soul). ||6||

Nara-Narayan sarisa subhrātā |
Jag palak viseshi jan trata ||
Bhagati sutiya kala karan vibhooshan |
Jag hita hetu vimal vidhu pooshan ||7||

Good brothers like the divine sages Nara and Narayan, they are sustainers of the universe and redeemers of the devotees in particular. They are beautiful ornaments for the ears of the fair damsel in the form of Devotion personified and stand as the spotless son and moon for the good of the world. ||7||

Swād tosha sam sugati sudhā ke |
Kamath Shesh sam dhar vasudhā ke ||
Janamana manju kanja madhukar ke |
Jeeha Jasomati Hari Haladharke ||8||

They are like the taste and gratifying quality of nectar in the form of emancipation, and are supporters of the globe like the divine Tortoise and the Serpent god Shesha. Like the bees roaming about the minds-like the lotus - of the devotees, to the tongue -Yashoda- they are the two favourite names (that the tongue repeatedly chants,) Krishna and Balrama. ||8||

एक छत्रु एकु मुकुटमनि सब बरननि पर जोई।
तुलसी रघुवर नाम के वरन विराजत दोई।।९।।

तुलसीदास कहते हैं कि श्री राम के नाम के दोनों अक्षर बड़ी शोभा वाले हैं; जिनसे रकार (र) रेफ से और मकार मुकुटमणि अनुस्वार रूप से सब अक्षरों के ऊपर हैं। ।।९।।

समुझत सरिस नाम अरु नामी।
प्रीति परस्पर प्रभु अनुगामी।।
नाम रूप दुइ ईस उपाधी।
अकथ अनादि सुसामुझि साधी।।१०।।

समझने में नाम और नामी दोनों एक से हैं, किन्तु दोनों में परस्पर स्वामी और सेवक के समान प्रीति है। नाम और रूप दोनों ईश्वर की उपाधि हैं, ये दोनों (नाम और रूप) अनिर्वचनीय हैं, अनादि हैं और अच्छे ज्ञान से ही इनका स्वरूप समझ में आता है।।१०।।

को बड़-छोट कहत अपराधू।
सुनि गुन भेद समुझिहहिं साधू।।
देखि अहिं रूप नाम अधीना।
रूप ग्यान नहिं नाम विहीना।।११।।

दोनों में कौन छोटा है और कौन बड़ा, यह कहना तो अपराध है। इनके गुणों का भेद सुनकर विज्ञ (साधु) पुरुष स्वयं ही समझ लेंगे। रूप को नाम के अधीन देखा जाता है, नाम के बिना रूप का ज्ञान संभव नहीं हो सकता।।११।।

Eka chhatra eku mukutamani sab baranani par joi |

Tulsi Raghuvar Nām ke, baran birājat doi ||9||

Tulsidas says that the two letters of Lord Ram's name have their own glory; the one spreads like an umbrella and the other resting like a crown jewel[1] . ||9||

Sammujhat sarisa nām aru nāmi |

Preeti paraspara Prabhu anugāmi ||

Nam roop dui eesha upādhee |

Akatha anādi susā mujhi sādhee ||10||

The name and the object named, though similar in significance, are allied as master and servant to one another. [As the name precedes the object of the person]. Name and form are two attributes of God, yet both of them are ineffable and beginning-less and can be rightly understood with noble knowledge. ||10||

Ko barh chhota kahat aparādhoo |

Suni guni bheda samujhihen sādhoo ||

Deekhiahin roop nam adheena |

Roop gyān nahin nām viheena ||11||

It is tantamount to committing a crime to brand one as superior and the other as inferior. However, discerning the subtle difference in their description the learned would know it themselves. Form is generally held dependent upon the form, for, without name the form cannot be even visualised (in absence). ||11||

---

1. 'Ra' in Nagari script is also written as Hindi sound kZ and 'Ma' is like the dot over the line when conjoined with other words.

रूप बिसेष नाम बिनु जाने।
करतल गत न परहिं पहिचाने॥
सुमिरिअ नाम रूप बिनु देखें।
आवत हृदय सनेह बिसेषें॥१२!!

कोई-सा भी विशेष रूप, उसका नाम जाने बिना चाहे हथेली पर ही क्यों न रखा हो उसे पहिचाना नहीं जा सकता और रूप के देखे बिना भी यदि नाम का स्मरण किया जाए तो विशेष प्रेम के कारण वह स्वतः हृदय में आ जाता है। ॥१२॥

नाम रूप गति अकथ कहानी।
समुझत सुखद न परति बखानी॥
अगुन सगुन बिच नाम सुखानी।
उभय प्रबोधक चतुर दुभाखी॥१३॥

नाम और रूप की गति की कथा अकथनीय है। वह समझने में सुखदायक है, परन्तु उसका वर्णन संभव नहीं है। श्रीराम का नाम निर्गुण और सगुण के मध्य सुन्दर साक्षी है, और उनका यथार्थ ज्ञान कराने वाला चतुर दुभाषिया है। ॥१३॥

राम नाम मनिदीप धरू जीह देहरीं द्वार।
तुलसी भीतर बाहेरहुँ जो चाहसि उजियारा॥१४॥

तुलसीदास कहते हैं, यदि तुम (भक्त) भीतर और बाहर, दोनों ओर उजाला चाहते हो तो मुख रूपी द्वार की जीव रूपी देहरी पर राम-नाम रूपी मणि दीप को रखो। ॥१४!!

Roop vishesha nām binu jane |
Kartal gata na parahin pahichane ||
Sumiria nām roop binu dekhen |
Āwat hridayan sānch bishesen ||12||

Typical forms cannot be identified, even if they be in your hand, without knowing their name. And if the name is remembered even without seeing the form, the latter flashes on the mind with a special liking for it. ||12||

Nām roop gati akatha kahānee |
Samujhat sukhad na parat bakhānee ||
Aguna saguna bich nām susākhee |
Ubhaya prabodhak chatur dubhakhee ||13||

The mystery of name and form is a tale which cannot be told, though delightful to comprehend yet difficult to describe. Between the unqualified Absolute and qualified Divinity, the Name is a good intermediary; it is a clever interpreter revealing the truth of both. ||13||

Rām nām manideep dharu jeeha dehareen dwār |
Tulsi bheetar bahirehu jo chahasi ujiyār ||14||

Tulsidas says: Install the luminous gem in the shape of Lord Ram's name on the threshold of the tongue at the doorway of your mouth if you desire light both within and without. ||14||

नाम जीहँ जपि जागहिं जोगी।
बिरत बिरंचि प्रपंच वियोगी।।
ब्रह्म सुखहिं अनुभवहिं अनूपा।
अकथ अनामय नाम न रूपा।।१५।।

श्री ब्रह्माजी द्वारा निर्मित इस प्रपंच से भलीभाँति विरत वैराग्यवान् मुक्त योगी पुरुष इस नाम को ही जीभ से जपते हुए जागते हैं तथा नाम रूप से रहित अनुपम, अनिर्वचनीय, अनामय ब्रह्मसुख का अनुभव करते हैं। ।।१५।।

जाना चहहिं गूढ़ गति जेऊ।
नाम जीहँ जपि जानहिं तेऊ।
साधक नाम जपहिं लय लाएँ।
होहिं सिद्ध अनिमादिक पाएँ।।१६।।

जो परमात्मा के गूढ़ रहस्य की महिमा को जानना चाहते हैं वे भी नाम को जीभ से जपकर उसका ज्ञान कर लेते हैं। साधक जन लौ लगाकर नाम का जप करते हैं और अणिमादि सिद्धियों को पाकर सिद्ध हो जाते हैं। ।।१६।।

जपहिं नाम जन आरत भारी।
मिटहिं कुसंकट होहिं सुखारी।।
राम भगत जग चारि प्रकारा।
सुकृति चाहिउ अनघ उदारा।। ।।१७।।

आर्त भक्त नाम जप करते हैं तो उनके भारी से भारी संकट समाप्त हो जाते हैं और वे सुखी हो जाते हैं। संसार में चार प्रकार[1] के राम भक्त हैं। और ये चारों ही पुण्यात्मा, पापरहित और उदार हैं। ।।१७।।

---

1. 'आर्त, अर्थार्थी, सत्यार्थी, ज्ञानी

Nam jeehan japi jagahin jogee |
Birat biranchi prapancha viyogee ||
Brahm sukhahin anubhavahim anoopā |
Akath anāmaya nām na roopā ||15||

Mystics who are full of dispassion and are wholly detached from God's creation keep aware (in the daylight of wisdom) muttering the name with their tongue and enjoy the felicity of Brahma (the absolute) which is beyond compare, beyond speech, sorrow, name or form. ||15||

Jana chahahin goodha gati jeuoo |
Nam jeehan japi janahi teuoo ||
Sadhak nām japahin laya lāyen |
Hohin siddha animadik pāyen ||16||

Strivers (hankering after worldly achievement) repeat the name, absorbed in contemplation, and become accomplished, acquiring super human powers[1] such as that of becoming infinitely small in size. ||16||

Japahin nam jan ārata bhāree |
Mitahin kusankat hohin sukhāree ||
Ram bhagat jag char prakārā |
Sukratee charahu anagh udārā ||17||

If the devoted in distress mutter the name, their worst calamities of the gravest type disappear and they become happy. In this world there are four kind of devotees[2] all the four of them are virtuous, sinless and noble or large-hearted. ||17||

---

1. They are eight in numbers. Read more about them ahead.
2. (i) distressed (ii) seekers of wealth (iii) seekers of truth (iv) the learned

चहू चतुर कहँ नाम अधारा।
ग्यानी प्रभुहि विसेषि पियारा॥
चहुँ जुग चहुँ श्रुति नाम प्रभाऊ।
कलि विसेषि नहिं आन उपाऊ॥१८॥

चारों ही चतुर भक्तों के लिए नाम ही एक मात्र आधार है, किन्तु इनमें ज्ञानी कोटि के भक्त प्रभु को विशेष रूप से प्रिय हैं। यों तो चारों युगों में और चारों ही वेदों में नाम का प्रभाव प्रकट हुआ है, किन्तु कलियुग में विशेष रूप से है। इस युग मे नाम के अलावा दूसरा कोई उपाय ही नहीं है। ॥८॥

सकल कामनाहीन जो राम भगति रस लीन।
नाम सुप्रेम पियूष हृद तिन्हुँ किए मन मीन॥ १९॥

जिन्हें किसी भी प्रकार की कामना नहीं है और जो श्री रामचन्द्र जी की भक्ति के रस में लीन हैं उन्होंने भी नाम के सुन्दर प्रेम रूपी अमृत के सरोवर में अपने मन को मछली बना रखा है। ॥१९॥

नामु राम को कल्पत कलि कल्यान निवासु।
जेहि सुमिरत भयो भाँग से तुलसी तुलसीदासु । ॥२०॥

श्रीराम का नाम कलियुग में कल्पवृक्ष और कल्याण का आवास (मुक्ति का घर) है, जिसके स्मरण करने से 'भाँग' जैसा तुलसीदास 'तुलसी' के समान पवित्र हो गया। ॥२०॥

Chahu chature kanha nām adhāra |
Gyani Prabhuhi vishesh piyārā ||
Chahun jug chahun shruti nām prabhaoo |
Kali vishesi nahin ān upaoo ||18||

All the four, clever as they are, rely upon the Name. Of these the enlightened devotee is specially dear to the Lord. The glory of the Name is supreme in all the four Yugas and all the four Vedas, particularly in the Kali Yug (Age) in which there is no other alternative either. ||18||

Sakal kamanā heen je Ram bhagati ras leen |
Nām suprema piyoosh hrida tinhoon kiye man meen ||19||

Even those who are free from all desires and absorbed in the joy of devotion to Lord Ram have thrown their heart as fish into the nectarine lake of supreme affection for thc Name. ||19||

Namu Ram ko kalpataru, Kali kalyan niwāsa |
Jehi sumirat bhayo bhāng te tulasi Tulsidās ||20||

The name of Ram is a wish-yielding tree, the very abode of beatitude in this age of Kali, by remembering which Tulsidas was transformed from Bhang (hemp) plant into the holy basil. ||20||

Note: [These Chaupayees are not taken in the same order as in the text]

श्री राम-आरती

श्रीरामचन्द्र कृपालु भज मन, हरण भवमय दारुणं।
नवकंज-लोचन कंजमुख, कर-कंज,पद कंजारुणं।।
कन्दर्प अगणित अमित छवि, नवनील-नीरद सुन्दरं।
पट पीत मानहु तड़ित रुचि-शुचि नौमि जनक सुतावरं।।
भजु दीन बन्धु दिनेश दानव, दैत्य-वंश-निकन्दनं।
रघुनन्द आनंदकन्द कौशल चन्द दशरथ-नंदनं।।
सिर मुकुट कुण्डल तिलक चारु उदार अंग विभूषणं।
आजानुभुज शर-चाप-धर संग्राम-जित खरदूषणं।।
इति वदित तुलसीदास शंकर-शेष-मुनि-मन रंजनं।
मम हृदय-कंज निवास कुरु, कामादि खल-दल गंजनं।।

हे मन! तू भक्तों पर कृपा करने वाले श्री रामचन्द्र जी की अर्चना कर जो भवसागर से दारूण (भयंकर) भयों (परेशानियों) को दूर करने वाले हैं। उनकी आँखें नए उगे कमल की भाँति हैं, कमल जैसा ही उनका चेहरा है। हाथ भी कमल रूपी हैं और पाँव ऐसे हैं मानों गहरे लाल कमल खिल रहे हों। असंख्य कामदेवों को लजाने वाली वह असीमित छवि ऐसी प्रतीत होती है मानो श्यामवर्णी बादलों का कोई मनोहारी रूप हो। उस पर पीताम्बर की छटा मानों बादलों को आच्छदित करने वाली विद्युत की तरह परम-पवित्रता से द्युतिमान है। हे मन! तू आनन्द के पुंज, रघु के वंशज, कौशल की कीर्ति और दशरथ के नन्दन (श्रीराम) को भज जो समस्त दैत्यों -दानवों के वंशों द्वारा फैलाए अंधकार को दूर करने वाले सूर्य हैं। उनके शीश पर मुकुट और तिलक है, कानों में कुण्डल उनके विशाल और दर्शनीय अंग आभूषणों से युक्त हैं। उनके घुटनों तक पहुँचने वाली भुजाओं में धनुष और बाण सुशोभित हैं जिनके द्वारा उन्होंने संग्राम में खरदूषण को जीत लिया था। तुलसीदास कहते हैं कि श्रीराम का यह स्वरूप शंकर, शेषनाग तथा मुनियों के हृदयों को आनन्द प्रदान करने वाला है। उनकी प्रार्थना है कि काम एवं अन्य बुराइयों का शमन करने वाला यह रूप उनके (तुलसीदास) हृदयरूपी कमल में सदा निवास करे।

(viii) Lord Ram's Arti

Shree-Rāmchandra kripalu bhaj man, haran bhav-bhaya dārunam |
Navakanj-lochan, kanjamukh, kar-kanj, pada kanjārunam | |
Kandarp aganita amita chhavi, navneela-neerad sundaram |
Pata peeta manahu tarhita ruchi-suchi naumi Janakasutā varam |
Bhaju deena bandhu dinesh dānav, daitya-vansha-nikandanam | |
Raghunanda anandakanda kaushal chanda Dashrathanandanam | |
Sir mukut kundal tilak charu udār ang vibhushnam |
Ājanubhuj shar-chap-dhar sangrām-jit-Khar-Dooshanam | |
Iti vadati Tulsidās Shankar-shesh-muni-man-ranjanam |
Mam hridaya-kunj niwās kuru, kamādi khal-dal ganjanam | |

O Mind! Worship Lord Ram who is ever gracious to his devotees and whose grace can destroy the most deadly mundane afflictions and fears. He whose eyes look like a nascently blooming lotus and face like the lotus flower. His hands are as beautiful as the lotus and his feet appear like (two) deep red lotus flowers, abloom. His this appearance of him which goes beyond the extent of vision, also pales into insignificance the combined charm of innumerable Kaam-Dev and gives the impression of a dark nimbus, with his yellow raiment appearing like the streak of lightning, pure and neat. I bow to such captivating appearance of Janaka's daughter, Sita's groom. O Mind! Ever worship the beacon on his head; he has large ear-rings and his well endowed body has ornaments adorning its various limbs in a sleek fashion. His long arms which reach upto his knees has the bow and arrow with which he vanquished Khara and Dooshan, the demons. Says Tulsidas that his this form is very captivating to Shankar, Sheshnag and sages which gives them supreme delight. The poet (Tulsidas) prays: may this form which destroys all evils like passion and lust ever dwell in his heart's lotus!

देवों द्वारा भगवान विष्णु की स्तुति
(तुलसीकृत श्री रामचरितमानस से)

जय जय सुरनायक जन सुखदायक प्रनतपाल भगवंता
गो द्विज हितकारी जय असुरारी सिंधुसुता प्रिय कंता॥
पालन सुर धरनी अद्भुत करनी मरम न जानइ कोई।
जो सहज कृपाला दीन दयाला करहु अनुग्रह सोई॥

हे देवताओं के नायक, भक्तजनों को सुख देने वाले, शरणागत की रक्षा करने वाले भगवान! आपकी जय हो! जय हो! हे गौ तथा ब्राह्मण का हित करने वाले, असुरों का विनाश करने वाले, समुद्र की कन्या (लक्ष्मी जी) के प्रिय स्वामी! आपकी जय हो। हे देवता और पृथ्वी के पालन करने वाले (जगदीश)! आपकी करनी अद्भुत है जिसका मार्ग कोई नहीं जानता। ऐसे जो स्वभाव से कृपालु और दीनों पर दया करने वाले हैं- वे ही हम पर कृपा करें।

जय-जय अविनासी सब घटबासी व्यापक परमानन्दा।
अविगत गोतीतं चरित पुनीतं माया रहित मुकन्दा॥
जेहि लागि बिरागी अति अनुरागी बिगत गोह मुनिवृन्दा।
निसि बासर ध्यावहिं गुन गन गावहिं जयति सच्चिदानन्दा॥

हे अविनाशी, सबके हृदय में निवास करने वाले अन्तर्यामी, सर्वव्यापक परमानन्द स्वरूप, अज्ञेय, इन्द्रियों से परे, पवित्र-चरित्र, माया से रहित मोक्षदाता! आपकी जय हो! जय हो! जिसे इस लोक और परलोक सबके भोगों से विरक्त तथा विगतमोह मुनिवृन्द भी अत्यंत अनुराग से रात-दिन जिनका ध्यान करते हैं और जिनके गुणों के समूह का गान करते हैं-उन सच्चिादानन्द की जय हो!

(ix) God's prayer to Lord Vishnu
(From Tulsidas's Sriramcharit manas)

Jai Jai Suranāyak jan sukhdāyak pranatapāl
Bhagwantā |
Go dwij hitakari jai asurari Sindhusutā priyā kantā ||
Pālan sur dharani, adbhuta karani maram na janei koi |
Jo sahaj kripalā deenadayalā karahu anugraha soi ||

Victory! Victory to thee, O Master of gods! Bestower of happiness to his devotees and protector of the faithful! Supreme Lord! Victory to thee! O benefactor of the brahmans and cow, foe of the demon, beloved spouse of the daughter of sea (Lakshmi). O preserver of the earth and goddom! Your supportive acts are amazing for no body knows their secret. He who by nature kind and compassionate to the humble, may show His favour to us!

Jai jai avināsi sab ghat bāsi vyapak parmanandā |
Avigat goteetam charita puneetam maya rahit
Mukundā ||
Jehi lāgi birāgi ati anurāgi vigat moh muni vrindā |
Nisi bāsar dhyāvahin gun gan gāvahi jayati
sacchidanandā ||

Victory, victory to thee O Imperishable, pervading in all hearts, omnipresent, the embodiment of supreme bliss, beyond comprehension, transcending the range of senses, doer of the pious deeds, devoid of all illusions and the bestower of the final release victory to thee! He, who is contemplated upon lovingly day and night by the great saints who having past their ignorance and completely detached from the attractions of this and the other world-whose glory is sung by them incessantly. victory to the True Being, the conscious, the perfect Bliss!

जेहि सृष्टि उपाई त्रिबिध बनाई संग सहाय न दूजा।
जो करहु अघारी चिंत हमारी जानिअ भगति न पूजा।।
जो भव भय भंजन मुनि मन रंजन गंजन विपत्ति बरूथा।
मन बच क्रम बानी छाड़ि सयानी सकल सुर जूथा।।

जिन्होंने बिना किसी सहायक या साथी के अकेले ही तीन प्रकार[1] की सृष्टि का निर्माण किया, वे पापों का अन्त करने वाले भगवान हमारी सुधि लें। हम न तो भक्ति जानते हैं, न ही हमें पूजा- विधि का ज्ञान है। जो संसार से भय का नाश करने वाले, मुनियों के मन को आनन्द देने वाले और विपत्तियों के समूह का नाश करने वाले हैं-हम सब देवताओं के समूह, मन-वचन और कर्म से चतुराई करने का प्रयत्न छोड़ कर उन भगवान की शरण आए हैं।

सारद श्रुति सेषा रिषय असेषा जा कहुँ कोउ नहिं जाना।
जेहि दीन पियारे वेद पुकारे द्रवउ सो श्री भगवाना।।
भव वारिधि मंदर सब विधि-सुन्दर गुनमंदिर सुखपुंजा।।
मुनि सिद्ध सकल सुर परम भयातुर नमत नाथ पद कंजा।।

सरस्वती, वेद और शेष जी तथा सारे ऋषि-मुनि-कोई भी-जिनको जानने-समझने में असमर्थ रहते हैं; जिन्हें दीन प्रिय हैं- ऐसा वेदों का कथन है-वे ही भगवान हम पर दया करें। हे संसार रूपी समुद्र के मथने के लिए मन्दराचल रूप, सब प्रकार से सुन्दर, गुणों के धाम और सुख की राशि-हे नाथ! आपके चरण कमलों में मुनि सिद्ध और सारे देवता भय से व्याकुल होकर-नमस्कार करते है।

---

1. 'सात्विक, राजसिक एवम् तामसिक

Jehi shrishti upāyee trividha banayee sang sahāya na dooja |
So karahu aghāri chinta hamāri janiya bhagati na poojā |
Jo bhav bhaya bhanjan muni man ranjan ganjan vipati varoothā
Manṭvacha kram bani chharhi sayani saran sakal sur joothā |

May he, who without any aid brought to birth the three creation;[1] the destroyer of sin, hear our cry for succour for we know no devotion or means of worship. The one who snaps the shackles of mundane fears; who is a source of delight to the sages' mind and who is the destroyer of all calamities - listen! We, the whole company of gods have come to thee for refuge, abandoning the skill of speech in thought, word and deed [as we failed miserably when we employed our these faculties to redeem our distress].

Sārad shruti Shesha rishaya aseshā ja kahun kou nahin jāna |
Jehi deena piyāre veda pukāre, dravahu so shree Bhagawāna | |
Bhava vāridha mandar sab vidhi sundar gunamandir sukha-punja |
Muni siddha sakal sur param bhayatur namat nath pad kanja |

May he whom Sharada[2], the scriptures, Shesha (the serpent) and all the seers cannot comprehend, he to who all distressed are dear-so declare the Vedas-thaw with mercy upon us! O Great God! O Mandar (hill) to churn the sea of mundane existence, in all ways comely, shrine of perfection and beacon of joy, listen! All the sages, seers, adepts and gods in dire affright do reverence, O Lord, to your lotus feet.

1. The three categories of the entire creation are (i) Sāttvik (noble), (ii) Rājas (passionate) and (iii) Tāmas (dull)

2. Goddess of Wisdom and Speech, Saraswati.

विष्णु-रूप राम का ऋषि द्वारा स्तवन
(तुलसीकृत श्री रामचरितमानस से)

नमामि भक्त वत्सलं। कृपालु शील कोमलं।।
भजामि ते पदाम्बुजं। अकामिनां स्वधामदं।।

हे भक्तवत्सल! हे कृपालु! हे कोमल स्वभाव वाले! आपको मैं नमस्कार करता हूँ। निष्काम पुरुषों को अपना परमधाम देने वाले! मैं आपको चरणों को भजता (वन्दना) करता हूँ।

निकाम श्याम सुन्दरं। भवाम्बुनाथ मंदरं।।
प्रफुल्ल कंज लोचनं। मदादि दोष मोचनं।।

आप नितान्त सुन्दर, श्याम, संसार-रूपी समुद्र को मथने के लिए मन्दराचल रूप, फूले हुए कमल के समान नेत्रों वाले और मद आदि दोषों को छुड़ाने वाले हैं।

प्रलंब बाहु विक्रमं। प्रभोऽप्रमेय वैभवं।।
निषंग चाप सायकं। धरं त्रिलोक नायकं।।

हे प्रभो! आपकी लम्बी भुजाओं का पराक्रम और आपका ऐश्वर्य बुद्धि के परे अथवा असीम है। आप तरकस और धनुषबाण धारण करने वाले, तीनों लोकों के स्वामी-

(x) An Eulogy by a Sage to Lord Vishnu's Incarnation as Ram

(From Tulsidas's 'Sriramcharita manas')

Namāmi bhakta vatsalam | Kripālu sheela komalam ||
Bhajāmi te padambujam | Akaminām swadhāmadam ||

I revere you, who are so fond of your devotees; kind and gentle of disposition. I adore your lotus feet, which vouchsafe to your selfless devotees a place in your own abode.

Nikam shyām sundaram | Bhavambunāth mandaram ||
Prafulla kunja lochanam | Madadi dosha mochanam ||

You have an exquisitely beautiful form; you are Mount Mandar, as it were, to churn the ocean of mundane existence; you have eyes like the full-blown lotus and you rid your votaries of pride and other vices.

Pralamba bāhu vikramam | Prabhoā prameya
Vaibhāvam ||

Nishangā Chap sāyakam | Dharam triloka nāyakam ||
Immense is the might of your long arms and immeasurable is your glory. You carry on your person a quiver, a bow and an arrow, O Lord of the three realms.

दिनेश वंश मंडनं। महेश चाप खंडनं।।
मुनीन्द्र संत रंजनं। सुरारि वृन्द भंजनं।।

(श्री राम के रूप में) सूर्यवंश के भूषण, शिव जी का धनुष तोड़ने वाले, मुनियों और संतो को आनन्द देने वाले तथा देवताओं के शत्रु-समूह का नाश करने वाले हैं।

मनोज वैरि वंदितं। अजादि देव सेवितं।।
विशुद्ध बोध विग्रहं । समस्त दूषणापहं।।

आप कामदेव के शत्रु शिवजी द्वारा वंदित, ब्रह्मा आदि देवताओं द्वारा सेवित, विशुद्ध ज्ञान की मूर्ति और समस्त दोषों को नष्ट करने वाले हैं।

नमामि इंदिरा पतिं। सुखाकरं सतां गतिं।।
भजे सशक्ति सानुजं। शची पति प्रियानुजं।।

हे लक्ष्मीपते! मैं आपको नमस्कार करता हूँ। आप सुखों की खान और सत्पुरुषों की गति हो। हे इन्द्र के प्रिय छोटे भाई[1] ! श्री सीता जी और छोटे भाई लक्ष्मण जी सहित मैं (आपके राम रूप) को भजता हूँ।

---

1. 'पौराणिक मान्यता के अनुसार देव माता अदिति के गर्भ से पहले इन्द्र का जन्म हुआ और बाद में विष्णु का इसलिए विष्णु इन्द्र के छोटे भाई हुए।

Dinesh vansha mandanam |Mahesha chāp khandanam ||
Muneendra sant ranjanam |Surari vrinda bhanjanam ||

The ornament of the solar race (in the form of Ram), You broke the bow of Lord Shiv. Delighting the greatest sages and saints, you crushed a host of demons (who are the enemy of gods).

Manoj vairi vanditam |Ajādi deva sevitam ||
Vishudha bodha vigraham |Samasta dooshanapaham ||

You are an object of reverence to the enemy of god of love (or Lord Shiv), and are adored by Brahma and other divinities. An embodiment of pure consciousness. You destroy all evils.

Namami Indirā patim |Sukhākaram satam gatim ||
Bhaje sashakti sānujam |Shachee pati priyanujam ||

I bow to Lakshmi's Lord, the fountain of joy and salvation of saints. I adore you with your spouse and younger brother (Lakshman). You are yourself a beloved younger brother[1] of Indra (Shachi's Lord).

---

1. Mythologically Vishnu is the younger brother of Indra. Both have their common mother, Aditi the mother of all gods.

त्वदंघ्रि मूल ये नराः। भजंति हीन मत्सराः।।
पतंति नो भवार्ण वे। वितर्क वीचि संकुले।।

जो मनुष्य छल-कपट से रहित हो कर आपके चरण-कमलों का सेवन करते हैं, वे अनेक प्रकार के सन्देह-रूपी तरंगों से पूर्ण संसार-रूपी समुद्र में नहीं गिरते।

विविक्त वासिनः सदा। भजंति मुक्तये मुदा।।
निरस्य इन्द्रियादिकं। प्रयांति ते गतिं स्वकं।।

जो एकान्त वासी पुरुष मुक्ति की आशा से, इन्द्रिय-सुख छोड़कर, प्रसन्नता-पूर्वक आपको भजते हैं, वे आपकी गति को प्राप्त होते हैं।

तमेकमदभुतं प्रभुं। निरीहमीश्वरं विभुं।
जगदगुरुं च शाश्वतं । तुरीयमेव केवलं।।

आपको (आपकी गति को) जो एक, अद्भुत, सर्वसमर्थ, इच्छारहित, ईश्वर, व्यापक, जगद्गुरु, सनातन, तीनों गुणों से सर्वथा परे और केवल अपने स्वरूप में स्थित हैं।

Tvadanghra moola ye narah |Bhajante heen matsarah ||
Patanti no bhavarna ve |Vitarka veechi sankule ||

Men who worship (even) the sole of your feet without any malice or guile in their hearts sink not into the ocean of metempsychosis, turbulent with the bellows of wrangling.

Vivakta vasinah sada |Bhajanti muktye mudā ||
Nirasya indiryādikam |Prayanti te gatim swakam ||

They who, living in seclusion, constantly worship you with their senses and mind fully subdued for the sake of attaining liberation are able to realise their own self.

Tamekamabhutam prabhum | Nireehameeshwaram vibhum ||
Jagadgurum cha shāshwatam |Tureeyameva kewalam ||

I adore Him, the mysterious Lord, who is unique, desireless, all powerful and omnipresent, the teacher of the world, eternal, transcending the three Attributes and Absolute (or self-existent).

भजामि भाव वल्लभं। कुयोगिनां सुदुर्लभं।।
स्वभक्त कल्प पादपं। समं सुसेव्यमन्वहं।।

जो भाव कुयोगियों के लिए दुलर्भ, अपने भक्तों के लिए कल्पवृक्ष सम और सदा सुखपूर्वक सेवन करने योग्य है-मैं निरंतर भजता हूँ।

अनूप रूप भूपतिं। नतोऽहमुर्विजापतिं।।
प्रसीद से नमामि ते। पदाबज भक्ति देहि में।।

हे अनुपम सुन्दर! हे पृथ्वीपते! हे जानकीनाथ। मैं तुमको प्रणाम करता हूँ। मुझ पर प्रसन्न होइए-मैं आपको नमस्कार करता हूँ। अपने चरण कमलों की भक्ति मुझे दीजिए।

पठंति ये स्तवं इदं। नरादरेण ते पदं।।
प्रजंति नात्र संशयं । त्वदीय भक्ति संयुता।।

जो मनुष्य आदरपूर्वक इस स्तुति को पढ़ते हैं, आपकी भक्ति से संयुत होकर वे आपके परमपद को प्राप्त होते हैं-इसमें सन्देह नहीं ।

Bhajami bhavvallabham |Kuyoginam sudurlabham ||
Swabhakta kalpa pādapam |Samam susevyamanvaham ||

I adore him who is fond of devotion, who is most difficult to access to the sensuous-minded seekers but who is a wish yielding tree to His own devotees; who is Impartial and so easy to worship.

Aroopa roop bhoopatim | Natohnurvijapatim ||
Praseeda me namami te | Padabje bhakti dehi me ||

I bow to Sita's lord, incomparably handsome and the Master of the earth. I reverence you; be gracious to me and grant me devotion to your lotus feet.

Pathanti ye stvam idam | Narādarena te padam ||
Vrajanti natra samshayam | Twadeeya bhakti samyuta ||

Men who recite this hymn with reverence undoubtedly attain your abode with unseperable devotion to your feetṭthere is no doubt about it.

श्री हनुमान चालीसा

(तुलसीकृत)

दोहा: श्री गुरु चरन सरोज रज, निजमन मुकुरु सुधारि।
बरनउँ रघुवर विमल जसु जो दायकु फल चारि।।

श्री गुरु महाराज के चरण कमलों की धूलि से अपने मन रूपी दर्पण को पवित्र कर के श्री रघुवीर के निर्मल यश का वर्णन करता हूँ जो चारों फल (धर्म, अर्थ, काम और मोक्ष) देने वाला है।

दोहा: बुद्धिहीन तनु जानि के, सुमिरों पवन-कुमार।
बल बुद्धि विद्या देहु मोहि, हरहु कलेश विकार।।

हे पवन कुमार! मैं आपका स्मरण करता हूँ। आप तो जानते है कि मेरा शरीर और बुद्धि निर्बल है। मुझे शारीरिक बल, सद्‌बुद्धि एवम् ज्ञान दीजिए और-मेरे दुःखों व दोषों का नाश कीजिए।

चौपाई: जय हनुमान ज्ञान गुन सागर।
जय कपीस तिहुँ लोक उजागर।।१ ।।

हे हनुमान जी! आपकी जय हो। आपका ज्ञान और गुण अथाह है। हे कपीश्वर! आपकी जय हो। तीनों लोकों (स्वर्ग, भू-लोक और पाताल लोक) में आपकी कीर्ति है। ।।१ ।।

रामदूत अतुलित बल धामा।
अंजनि-पुत्र पवनसुत नामा ।।२।।

हे पवन सुत! हे अंजनी नन्दन! हे श्री राम के दूत! आपके समान दूसरा बलवान नहीं है। ।।२।।

(xi) Forty Rhymes in the Honour of Lord Hanuman (By Tulsidas)

Doha: Shree guru charan saroj raj, nij man mukur sudhāri |
Barnau Raghuvar vimal jasu, jo dāyak phal chari ||

Having cleaned my mind's mirror by the dust of my guru's feet-like the pollen of the lotus flower, I now attempt to describe the noble glory of Lord Ram who is the bestower of all the four fruitful rewards: the righteous behaviour, fulfillment of material want, and of desires and the final salvation of soul.

Doha: Buddhiheen tanu jāniken, sumiron Pavan-kumār |
Bal, budhi, vidyā dehu mohi, harahu kalesh vikār ||

But since I am weak in body and mind, I invoke your blessings, O son of the Wind-God! Kindly grant me the physical and mental power, righteous wisdom and knowledge and end my sorrows and afflictions so that I may accomplish what I want!

Chaupai: Jai Hanuman gyān gun sāgar |
Jai kapees ṭihun lok ujāgar ||1||

Victory to thee, O Lord Hanuman. Your knowledge and wisdom is unfathomable. O Lord of Monkeys! Victory to thee! All the three worlds (heaven, earth and the nether world) are instinct with your glory.

Ram doot atulit bal dhāmā |
Anjani-putra Pavan-sut nama ||2||

O Son of the Wind-god! O Son of Mother Anjani! O Messenger of Lord Ram! No one is more powerful than you |

महावीर विक्रम बजरंगी।
कुमति निवार सुमति के संगी ।।३।।

हे महावीर बजरंग बली! आप विशेष पराक्रम वाले हैं। आप बुरी बुद्धि को दूर करते है और अच्छी बुद्धि वालों के साथी और सहायक होते हैं। ।।३।।

कंचन बरन विराज सुवेसा।
कानन कुण्डल कुन्जित केसा।।४।।

आपके शरीर का रंग सुवर्ण जैसा है। आपके कानों में कुण्डल है, और केश घुँघराले हैं। आपका सुवेष शोभा को प्राप्त हो रहा है। ।।४।।

हाथ वज्र और ध्वजा बिराजै! काँधे मूँज जनेउ साजै ।।५।।
संकर सुवन केसरी नंदन। तेज प्रताप महाजग वन्दन ।।६।।

आपके एक हाथ में वज्र (गदा) और दूसरे में ध्वजा शोभायमान है तथा कंध ो पर पड़ा हुआ मूँज का बना पवित्र यज्ञोपवीत शोभित हो रहा है। आप शंकर जी के पुत्र हैं तथा वानरराज केसरी के भी। आपका तेज और प्रताप महान है। आप संसार द्वारा वन्दना करने के योग्य हैं ।।५-६।।

विद्यावान गुनी अति चातुर। राम काज करिबे कौं आतुर।।७।।
प्रभु चरित्र सुनिबे कौ रसिया। राम लखन सीता मन बसिया।।८।।

आप विद्यावान गुणी और अति चतुर हैं तथा श्री राम का काम करने को सदैव अधीर रहते हैं। प्रभु श्री राम का चरित्र सुनते समय तो आप रसलीन हो जाते है। सीता, राम और लक्ष्मण आपके हृदय में तथा आप उनके हृदय में सदैव निवास करते हैं। ।।७-८।।

Mahaveer vikram Bajrangi |
Kumati niwar sumati ke sangi ||3||

O Supremely powerful! O Bajrang Bali[1]! You are capable of displaying great valour! You remove ignorance and help those with righteous wisdom and also remain with them.

Kanchan baran virāj suvesa |
Kanan kundal kunchitā kesa ||4||

Your body-hue is golden. You have curly hair and rings in the ears. Your comely appearance is enchanting ||4||

Hath Vajra aur dhwaja Virāje | Kandhe mooja janeu sāje ||5||

Sankar-suvan Kesari nandan | Tej pratāp maha jag-vandan ||6||

You weild a mace (like the thunderbolt) in one hand and a flag in the other. A holy thread made of the long reed lies upon your shoulder. You are the son of Lord Shankar and also of the Monkey Lord Kesari. Your glory and brilliance is illimitable and you deserve to be reverenced by the whole world. ||5-6||

Vidyavan guni ati chātur | Ram kaja karivey kou ātur ||7||

Prabhu charitra sunibey ko rasiyā | Ram-Lakhan-Sita man basiyā ||8||

You are supremely educated, wise and intelligent and ever ready to accomplish any job commanded by Lord Ram. You love listening to the doings of your Lord Ram and ever dwell in the hearts of Shree Ram, Lakshman, Sita and they dwell in your heart. ||7-8||

---

1. Literally meaning the one having limbs as powerful and sturdy as the thunder bolt.

सूक्ष्म रूप धरि सियहि दिखावा। विकट रूप धरि लंक जरावा।।९।।

भीम रूप धरि असुर संहारे। राम चन्द्र के काज सँवारे।।१०।।

सीता की खोज करने के लिए लंका में प्रवेश करते समय आपने सूक्ष्म रूप धारण कर लिया था। और सीता जी के सामने भी आप सूक्ष्म रूप में ही पहुँचे थे। लंका में राक्षसों का संहार करने के लिए आपने भयंकर रूप धारण कर लिया और लंका को जलाते समय आपका रूप बड़ा विकट हो गया था। इस प्रकार यथासमय यथावश्यक रूप धारण करते हुए आपने श्री राम की लीला के सब कार्यों को भली प्रकार संभाल लिया।।९-१०।।

Sookshma roop dhari Siyahi dikhava | Vikat roop dhari Lanka jarāvā ||9||

Bheem roop dhari Asur samhāre | Ram Chandra ke Kaja samvāre ||10||

While going in search of Sita to Lanka, You assumed a very tiny form and appeared before Sita in that very form. But when you burned Lanka you assumed a very big and dreadful form to slay the demon host. Thus, by your sheer intelligence you know how to present yourself on different occasions and thus managed to fulfil all the jobs assigned to you by Lord Ram. ||9-10||

लाइ सँजीवन लखन जियाए। श्री रघुवीर हरषि उर लाए।।११।।

रघुपति कीन्हीं बहुत बढ़ाई। तुम मम प्रिय भरतहिं सम भाई ।।१२।।

सहस बदन तुम्हरो जस गावें। अस कहि श्रीपति कंठ लगावें।।१३।।

सनकादिक ब्रह्मादिक मुनीसा। नारद सारद सहित अहीसा।।१४।।

जम कुबेर दिग्पाल जहाँते। कवि कोविद कहि सकहिं कहां ते।।१५।।

जब लंका की युद्धभूमि में शक्तिबाण के लगने से लक्ष्मण जी के लिए प्राणों का संकट उपस्थित हुआ था, तब आपने ही संजीवनी बूटी लाकर उनके प्राणों की रक्षा की थी। आपके इस कार्य से श्री राम इतने प्रभावित और हर्षित हुए कि स्नेह से भर कर उन्होंने आपको छाती से लगा लिया और आपकी बहुत प्रशंसा की। श्री प्रभु ने यहाँ तक कह दिया कि हे हनुमान! तुम मुझे भाई भरत के समान प्रिय हो। तुम्हारा यश इतना महान और विशाल है कि शेष नाग अपने सहस्त्र मुखों से नित्य गान किया करेंगे। सनकादि ब्रह्मनिष्ठ ऋषि, ब्रह्मादि देवता, नारदादि मुनीश्वर, स्वयं देवी शारदा (सरस्वती) एवम् शेष नाग, कुबेरादि सभी दिक्पाल, सभी कवि, कोविंद (विद्वान) तुम्हारा नित्य यशोगान करेंगे किन्तु फिर भी तुम्हारे यश को वह यथार्थ रूप में कह नहीं पाएंगे।।११-१५।।

Lāi sanjeevan Lakhan jiyaye | Shree Raghuvir harashi urlaye ||11||

Raghupati keenhee bahut badāi | Tum mum priya Bharatahi sam bhāyee ||12||

Sahas badan tumhro jas gāven | As Kahi Shreepati kantha lagāven ||13||

Sankadik Brahmadi muneeshā | Nārad Sārad sahita aheesa ||14||

Jam Kuber Digpāl jahān te | Kavi kobid kahi sakhi kahān te ||15||

When in the battlefield of Lanka, Lakshman ji was fatally wounded, it was you, O Lord Hanuman, who fetched the Sanjeevani Booti (Life reviving herb) and saved his life. Your this feat moved Lord Ram to tears, so much so that he embraced and praised you greatly. Your Lord Ram went to the extent of declaring you (Lord Hanuman) to be as dear to him as his own brother, Bharat. Your glory is so great and illimitable that even if the thousand hooded Serpent Shesha uses all its thousand mouths to describe it, he will fail to cover the total span. All the masters of the directions, the great seers and sages, Brahma and other gods, Kubera etc., all the great poets will ever go on describing your glory but they shall not succeed in fathoming the full aspects of your immense glory. ||11-15||

तुम उपकार सुग्रीवहि कीन्हा। राम मिलाई राज पद दीन्हा।।
तुम्हरो मंत्र विभीषण माना। लंकेश्वर भए सब जग जाना ।।१६-१७।।

हे हनुमान जी! आपने ही सुग्रीव की और श्री राम से मित्रता करवाई और उनको भयमुक्त कराकर उनका खोया हुआ राज्य दिलवाकर उनपर महान उपकार किया। लंका में जब आप सीता जी की खोज करने गये तो विभीषण से मिलते समय उन्हें आपने ही सलाह दी कि वह श्री राम की शरण में चले जांए। विभीषण ने इस सलाह को माना-फलस्वरूप उनके कष्ट ही दूर नहीं हुए, श्री राम कृपा से वह लंका के राजा बन गए-इस वृतान्त का सारा जग जानता है। ।।१६-१७।।

जुग सहस्र योजन पर भानू। लील्यो ताहि मधुर फल जानू।।
प्रभु मुद्रिका मेलि मुख माहिं। जलधि लाँघ गए अजरज नाहीं।।१८-१९।।

हे हनुमान जी, आपका अद्‌भुत पराक्रम आपके बचपन से ही प्रकट होने लगा था। तब आपने दो हजार योजन दूर आकाश में स्थित नवोदित सूर्य को लाल-मीठा फल समझकर पूरा मुख में रख लिया था। यह तो आपका बचपन में किया गया कृत्य था:फिर बड़े होने पर यदि श्री राम की दी हुई मुद्रिका को मुख में रखकर सौ योजन समुद्र को खेल-ही-खेल में पार कर आप लंका पहुँचे तो उसमें आश्चर्य की क्या बात है। ।।१८-१९।।

Tum upkār Sugreevahi keenha | Ram milai rāj pad deenhā |
Tumhro mantra Vibhishan mānā | Lankeshwar bhaye sab jag jānā ||16-17||

O Lord Hanuman! It was you who managed to establish friendship between Sugreeva and Lord Ram and thus made Sugreeva free of fear and ultimately he got back his lost kingdom. When you went to Lanka in Sita's search you met Vibhishan there and you suggested to him to seek shelter under Shree Ram's grace. Vibhishan heeded your advice and consequently got the kingship of Lanka besides the other religious merits owing to the grace of Lord Ram. The whole world knows well about your these tidings. ||16-17||

Jug Sahastra yojan par Bhānu! Leelyo tahi madhur phal jānu|
Prabhu mudrikā meli mukh mānhi! Jaladhi langha gaye achraj nāhi ||18-19||

O Lord Hanuman! Your marvellous prowess was manifest right since your childhood! Even then you just swallowed the morning sun, about a couple of thousands yojans away, deeming it to be a red-ripe fruit. Thus, when you grew up, you put the ring of Lord Ram inside your mouth and managed to leap across the sea some hundred yojan wide in a playful manner, to reach Lanka. You have been achieving these feats regularly so there is no surprise. ||18-19||

दुर्गम काज जगत के जेते। सुगम अनुग्रह तुम्हरे तेते॥२०॥

आपकी कृपा मात्र से संसार के सभी दुर्गम कार्य स्वतः सुगम हो जाते हैं। यह सब आपकी कृपा या अनुग्रह का ही कमाल है॥२०॥

राम दुआरे तुम रखवारे। होत न आज्ञा बिन पैसारे ॥२१॥

आप ही राम दरबार के द्वाररक्षक हो और आपकी आज्ञा के बिना भक्तों को राम-कृपा नहीं मिल सकती॥२१॥

सब सुख लहें तुम्हारी सरना। तुम रक्षक काहू को डरना॥२२॥

इस प्रकार संसार के सुख और सुविधाएं आपकी शरण में आने से ही मिलती हैं। यदि आप रक्षक हो तो फिर किसी को किसी भी चीज का डर नहीं रहता॥२२॥

आपन तेज सम्हारौ आपै। तीनहुँ लोक हाँक ते कांपे॥२३॥

आप ऐसे अद्वितीय तेजस्वी हो कि आप के तेज को आप स्वयं ही संभाल सकते हो-अन्य किसी को सामर्थ्य नहीं। आपकी हुँकार सुनकर तीनों लोक भय से काँप जाते हैं। ॥२३॥

Durgam kāj jagat ke jaite | Sugam anugraha tumhre tete ||20||

All the most difficult missions of the world become easily accomplishable by your grace. With your grace there is nothing in the world that cannot be accomplished. ||20||

Ram duāre tum rakhavāre| Hot na agya bin paisāre ||21||

You are the sentinel to the access to Lord Ram and without your support no aspirant can ever have the grace of Lord Ram. ||21||

Sab sukh lahen tumhāri sarana| Tum rakshak kāhoo ko darna ||22||

Thus, all the happiness and felicity of the world are achievable only when one seeks total refuge in your grace. With you being the protector, one need not be afraid of anything in the world. ||22||

Āpan tej samharo ape | Teenhhun lok hanka te kānpe ||23||

You are, O Lord, such supremely brilliant person that only you can control your illumitable power and prowess. None else can ever do so. Your one growl is enough to pulverise whole of the three worlds into fearful silence and all shudder to hear it. ||23||

भूत पिशाच निकट नहिं आवे। महावीर जब नाम सुनावै॥२४॥

आपका 'महावीर' नाम उच्चारित करते ही भूत पिशाच भाग जाते हैं और फिर पास भी नहीं फटकते॥२४॥

नासे रोग हरे सब पीरा। जपत निरंतर हनुमत वीरा॥२५॥

संकट ते हनुमान छुड़ावे। मन क्रम वचन ध्यान जो लावे॥२६॥

हे हनुमान जी! आप का नाम जपते ही सारे रोगों का नाश हो जाता है और सब पीड़ा दूर हो जाती है। अर्थात् जो मन, कर्म, वचन से आपका ध्यान अर्थात् स्मरण करते है, उनको आप सभी संकटों से मुक्त कर देते हैं। ॥२५-२६॥

सब पर राम तपस्वी राजा। तिनके काज सकल तुम साजा॥२७॥

श्री राम, जो कि परब्रह्म हैं ओर सर्वोपरि हैं, एक तपस्वी की भाँति निर्लिप्त भाव से राज करते हैं। उनको भी यदि (उनकी लीला के अन्तर्गत) कठिनाइयों का सामना करना पड़ा तो हे हनुमान! आपने ही उनको दूर किया था॥२७॥

Bhoot-pishāch nikat nahin āven! Mahavir jab nām sunāven ||24||

The moment one chants your name 'Mahavir' all the ghosts, goblins, hell-hounds flee away in panic, never to come back. ||24||

Nāse rog hare sab peerā | Japat nirantar Hanumat Veerā ||25||

Sankat te Hanuman chhudaven | Man kram vachan dhyān jo lāven ||26||

O Lord Hanuman! A mere chant of your name ends all affections and pains. If one devotes one's attention faithfully to your visage by word, deed and mind, you instantly remove all the obstructions and distress troubling him. ||25-26||

Sab par Ram tapasvi Rājā | Tin ke kaja sakal tum sājā ||27||

Lord Ram, the incarnation of the Supreme Being, is all powerful and Supreme and rules over the world dispassionately. But when he himself faced any problems in his wordly play, it was you always who solved them. ||27||

और मनोरथ जो कोई लावे। सोई अमित जीवन फल पावै॥२८॥

इस प्रकार कोई भी व्यक्ति यदि कोई मनोरथ या कामना लेकर आपकी शरण आता है तो उसकी कामना ही पूरी नहीं होती, आपकी कृपा से जीवन का असीम फल-भगवत्प्रेम भी प्राप्त हो जाता है। ॥२८॥

चारों जुग परताप तुम्हारा। है परसिद्ध जगत उजियारा॥२९॥

साधु संत के तुम रखवारे। असुर-निकंदन राम दुलारे॥३०॥

चारों युगों अर्थात् सतयुग, त्रेता, द्वापर और कलियुग में आपका प्रताप व्याप्त है और आपकी इस प्रसिद्धि से ही जगत में उजियाला-अर्थात् धार्मिकता-फैली रहती है। आप सदैव साधु संतों की रक्षा करते हैं। श्री राम के दुलारे आप साधु संतों और सज्जनों के रखवाले हैं और असुरों या राक्षसों का नाश करनेवाले हैं। ॥२९-३०॥

Aur manorath jo koi lāve | Soi amit jeevan phal pāve ||28||

Thus when anyone has any desire and seeks your shelter for its fulfillment, by your grace not only his desire gets fulfilled, he gets the ultimate fruit of lifeṭthe love for God Almighty as a bonus. ||28||

Charo yug partāp tumhara | Hai parsiddha jagat ujiyārā ||29||

Sadhu sant ke tum rakhware | Asur-nikandan Ram dulāre ||30||

Your glory, O Lord, premeates all the four ages: Satyug, Treta, Dwapar, and Kaliyug and owing to its pious light all the ages are radiant with the righteous grace. This is only because of you, O Lord! You always help noble persons, holy men, sages and seers and you achieve all this because you yourself are a darling devotee and servant of your Lord Ram. By His grace you slay all the demons and wicked tendencies in the world easily. ||29-30||

अष्टसिद्धि नवनिधि के दाता। असवर दीन्ह जानकी माता।।३१।।

राम-रसायन तुम्हरे पासा। सदा रहो रघुपति के दासा।।३२।।

आपको श्री जानकी माता से ऐसा वरदान मिला हुआ है कि आप किसी को भी आठों सिद्धियाँ और नौ निधियाँ[२] (अर्थात् सब प्रकार की सम्पत्ति और सुख) दे सकते है। आप निरंतर श्री राम जी की शरण में रहते हैं। जिससे आपके पास बुढ़ापा और असाध्य रोगों के नाश के लिए 'राम-नाम' रूपी औषधि रहती हैं । ।।३१-३२।।

---

२. नौ निधियाँ है: पद्म, महामद्म, शंख, मकर कच्छप, कुन्द, नील और बर्च्च (या खर्च) वह निधियाँ एक प्रकार की सख्याएँ हैं बेहद विशाल परिणाम में-अरबों खरबों से भी अधिक। अर्थात् कोई भी मनचाही वस्तु असीमित परिणाम में देने को श्री हनुमान सक्षम है जानकी माता के वरदान से।

आठ सिद्धियाँ निम्नलिखित है:

१	अणिमा	:	इससे साधक किसी को दिखाई नहीं पड़ता और वह कठिन से कठिन पदार्थ में प्रवेश कर सकता हैं।
२	महिमा	:	इससे योगी अपने आप को बहुत बड़ा कर सकता है।
३	गरिमा	:	इससे साधक अपने आपको चाहे जितना भारी बना सकता है।
४	लषिमा	:	इससे साधक जितना चाहे स्वयं को हलका कर सकता है।
५	प्राप्ति	:	मन चाहे पदार्थ को प्राप्त करने की सिद्धि ।
६	प्रकाम्ब	:	इससे साधक इच्छा करने पर पृथ्वी में समा सकता है या आकाश मे उड़ सकता है।
७	ईशित्व	:	इसके द्वारा साधक सब पर शासन करने के लिए समर्थ हो जाता है।
८	वशीत्व	:	इससे साधक किसी को भी अपने वश में कर लेता है।

Ashtha siddhi navniddhi ke dātā | As var deenha Jānaki Mātā ||31||

Ram-rasāyan tumhre pāsā | Sada raho Raghupati ke dāsā ||32||

You have received such a boon from mother Janaki as to empower you to grant the aspirant all the nine riches and eight perfections[2] (i.e., all the kinds of wealth and ability). You ever dwell in the shelter of Lord Ram and thus no illness or other worldly afflictions can ever touch you. It is because you have a Supreme-Drug, the love for Ram, ever with you. ||31-32||

---

2. The nine kinds of riches are: Padma, Mahapadma, Shankha, Makar, Kacchpa, Mukunda, Kunda, Neel and Barcha (or Kharva). These riches, actually indicate a very great number like billions and trillions. That is, Lord Hanuman, by the grace of the boon he received from mother Jānaki is capable of granting anything in any great quantity to his devotee.

The eight kinds of perfections are:

(i) Anima	:	This quality makes the aspirant invisible and capable of entering any substance easily.
(ii) Mahima	:	This makes the aspirant enhance his body to any size he wants.
(iii) Garima	:	This makes the aspirant grow as heavy as he wants.
(iv) Laghima	:	This makes the aspirant grow as light as he wants.
(v) Prapti	:	This makes the aspirant get anything he wants.
(vi) Prakamya	:	This makes the aspirant go inside the earth or fly in the sky at will.
(vii) Ishitva	:	This makes the aspirant rule over anything he wants.
(viii) Vashitva	:	This makes the aspirant control anything he wants.

तुम्हरे भजन राम को पावे। जनम-जनम के दुख बिसरावै॥३३॥

अन्तकाल रघुवर पुर जाई। जहाँ जनम हरि भक्ति कहाई॥३४॥

आपका भजन करने से श्री राम जी प्राप्त होते हैं और जन्म-जन्मान्तर के दुख दूर होते हैं और अन्त समय श्री रघुनाथ जी के धाम को जाते हैं-ऐसे लोग जब भी जन्म लेंगे तो राम के भक्त ही कहलाएंगे॥३३-३४॥

और देवता चित्त न धरई। हनुमत सेई सर्व सुख करई॥३५॥

हे हनुमान जी! आपकी सेवा करने से सब प्रकार के सुख मिलते हैं-फिर किसी अन्य देवता के पूजन की आवश्यकता ही नहीं रहती॥३५॥

संकट कटै मिटै सब पीरा। जो सुमिरे हनुमत बलबीरा॥३६॥

जो भी व्यक्ति बलशाली हनुमान जी का भजन करता है उसके सब कष्ट दूर हो जाते हैं और सारी पीड़ाएँ मिट जाती हैं॥३६॥

Tumhare bhajan Ram ko pāve | Janam-janam ke dukh bisrāve ||33||

Anta kal Rahguvar pur jāyee | Jahan janam Hari bhakta kahāyee ||34||

One who worships you also has his prayers answered by Lord Ram and thus all the afflictions accrued to one by a series of lives end. Such a man finally goes to the realm of Lord Ram and when he gets a new life, the devotion to Ram ever remains with him. Thus, he shall ever enjoy a privilege ensuring peace and prosperity in every life. ||33-34||

Aur devatā chitta na dharai | Hanumat sei sarva sukh karai ||35||

O Lord Hanuman! By doing service unto you the devotee gets every happiness and pleasure. Then he need not worship any other deity. ||35||

Sankat katey mitey sab peerā | Jo sumire Hanumat Balvirā ||36||

He who worships Lord Hanuman, supremely powerful, has all his troubles and afflictions end by the grace of the god. ||36||

जै जै जै हनुमान गौसाई। कृपा करहु गुरुदेव की नाई।।३७।।

हे हनुमान जी! आप हमारी सम्पूर्ण इन्द्रियों और शरीर तथा पूरे जीवन के मालिक है। आप हम पर ऐसी कृपा कीजिए जैसी कृपा गुरु शिष्य के ऊपर करते हैं। आपकी जय हो प्रभु, जय हो, जय हो।।३७।।

ये शत बार पाठ कर जोई। छूटहि बंदि महासुख होई।।३८।।

जो कोई इस हनुमान चालीसा का १०० बार पाठ करेगा वह सब बन्धनों से छूट जाएगा और उसे परमानन्द की प्राप्ति होगी।।३८।।

जो यह पढ़े हनुमान चालीसा। होय सिद्धि साखी गौरीसा।।३९।।

तुलसीदास सदा हरि चेरा। कीजे नाथ हृदय में डेरा।।४०।।

जो इस हनुमान चालीसा का पाठ करता है, शिव जी साक्षी हैं कि उसके कार्य सिद्ध होते हैं। तुलसीदास (इस 'हनुमान चालीसा' के रचियता) तो सदा ही हरि का सेवक हैं। हे हनुमान जी! आप उसके हृदय में सदा निवास करें ।।३९-४०।।

Jai jai jai Hanuman gusāeen | Kripa karahu gurudeva ki nāeen ||37||

O Lord Hanuman! You are the master of all our senses and body. Kindly show me your favour like a teacher shows on the disciple. O Lord, Victory to thee, Victory to thee, Victory to thee. ||37||

Ye shat bār path kar joee | Chhotahi bandi mahā sukh hoee ||38||

He who chants this 'Hanuman Chalisa' or the forty rhymes in the honour of Lord Hanuman) a hundred times shall be liberated to attain the highest status of his soul. ||38||

Jo yeh padhe Hanuman Chalisā | Hoye Siddhi Sakhi Gaureeshā ||39||

Tulsidas sada Hari cherā | Keeja Nath Hridaya men derā ||40||

Lord Shiva vouches for the fact the he who studies (or chants) this 'Hanuman Chalisa' a hundred times shall succeed in his every mission. Tulsidas (the creator of these panegyric rhymes) is ever a servant of Hari![3] O Lord Hanuman ! Kindly ever dwell in his heart. ||39-40||

---

3. An ephithet of Lord Vishnu but here it means Lord Ram who was an incarnation of Lord Vishnu.

दोहा: पवन-तनय संकट हरन, मंगल मूरति रूप।
रामलखन सीता सहित, हृदय बसहु सुरभूप।

हे संकटों के हरण करने वाले मंगल मूर्ति, देवों के राजा, हनुमान जी। मेरी आपसे प्रार्थना है कि आप श्रीराम, लक्ष्मण और सीता सहित मेरे हृदय में सदा निवास कीजिए।

Doha : Pavan-tanaya sankat haran, mangal moorati roop |
Ram-Lakhan-Seeta-Sahita, Hridaya basahu sur-bhoop |

O Remover of All Distress, O Auspicious-visaged, the Lord of the gods, Hanuman ji! I request you to ever dwell in my heart alongwith your chosen deity Lord Ram, his espouse Sita and his brother Lakshman.

संकट मोचन श्री हनुमानाष्टक

बाल समय रवि भक्ष लियौ, तब तीनहुँ लोक भयौ अँधियारो
ताहीं सौं त्रास भई जग को, यह संकट काहुसों जात न टारौ
देवन आइ करी बिनती, तब छाँड़ि दियौ रवि कष्ट निवारौ
को नहीं जानत है जग में, कपि संकट मोचन नाम तिहारौ॥१॥

अर्थ: हे हनुमान जी! बाल्यावस्था में एक दिन भूख लगने पर प्रातः काल उगते सूर्य को लाल-लाल मीठा फल समझ कर आपने मुँह में रख लिया था तो तीनों लोक अन्धकार में डूब गए थे और समस्त संसार भयभीत हो गया था। यह संकट किसी से टाला न जाता देख कर देवताओं ने जब आकर सूर्य को छोड़ देने की विनती की थी तो आपने सूर्य को मुक्त किया और सब का संकट दूर किया था। हे कपि! हे वानरराज! तुम्हारे संकट दूर करने वाले इस नाम और यश को संसार में कौन नहीं जानता॥१॥

(xii) The Eight Verses in the Honour of Hanuman, The Distress Dispeller

Bal samaya Ravi bhaksha liyo, tab teenahun lok bhayo andhiyāro
Tahi son trās bhayee jag kou, yeh sankat kahu son jat na tāro
Devan ani kari binati, tab chhāndi diyo ravi kashtha niwāro
Ko nahin jānat hai jag men, kapi sankat mochan nām tihāro ||1||

O Lord Hanuman! In your childhood, one day you felt very hungry in the early morning and deeming the rising sun to be some red-ripe fruit, you just flew up to it and swallowed it, causing darkness everywhere and the whole world was frightened. When no one could resolve this distressing situation, all the gods came to request you to release the sun from your mouth's cage. You did so and ended the distress of the world. O Great Monkey-lord, who does not know your capacity and renown to remove distress? ||1||

बालि की त्रास कपीस बसै गिरि, जात महाप्रभु पंथ निहारौ
चौकि महामुनि साप दियौ तब, चाहिए कौन उपाय बिचारौ
कै द्विज रूप लिआय महाप्रभु, सो तुम दास के सोक निवारौ
को नहिं जानत है जग में, कपि संकट मोचन नाम तिहारौ॥२॥

अर्थ: बालि से भयभीत कपीश सुग्रीव ऋष्यमूक पर्वत पर सुरक्षित था क्यों कि मुनि के शाप के भय से बालि वहाँ नहीं आ सकता था। एक बार दम्भ में बालि ने मतंग मुनि की तपस्या अनजाने में भंग की थी तब मुनि ने शाप दिया था कि यदि वह उनकी आराधना स्थली में आया तो नष्ट हो जाएगा। एक दिन महाप्रभु श्री राम को लक्ष्मण सहित उधर से आते हुए देखा तो सुग्रीव शंकित हुआ कि कहीं बालि ने अपने गुप्तचर तो नहीं भेजे है। तब सुग्रीव ने अपने प्रधान सांमत हनुमान जी को विप्ररूप धारण कर सत्य जानने को भेजा। हनुमान जी ने विशुद्ध संस्कृत में श्री राम-लक्ष्मण से परिचय प्राप्त किया और उन्हें सुग्रीव के पास लाकर उनकी मित्रता करवाई और इस प्रकार अंततः बालि का वध श्रीराम के हाथों कराकर सुग्रीव को त्रास से मुक्त किया। हे हनुमान जी आपके संकट दूर करने वाले नाम और यश को कौन नहीं जानता॥२॥

Bali ki trās kapees basei giri, jāt mahāprabhu pantha nihāro
Chonki Mahamuni sap diyo tab, chahiye kaun upaya bichāro
Kai dwij roop liayay Mahaprabhu, so tum das ke sok niwāro
Ko nahin jānat hai jag men, kapi sankat mochan nām tihāro ||2||

Afraid of the wrath of Bali, the Monkey king Sugreeva was dwelling on the Rishyamook Hill where Bali could not reach due to sage Matanga's curse [Once Bali, Sugreeva's elder brother, arrogantly disturbed the penance of the sage who cursed him that should he (Bali) reach his place of worship again, he shall die]. One day, sitting on the hill when Sugreeva saw Lord Ram coming with Lakshman, he thought Bali had sent these spies to kill him. Then Sugreeva asked you, Lord Hanuman to find out the truth. You went there in the garb of a brahman and conversed in chaste Sanskrit to get their introduction. Then you brought both the brothers and made Sugreeva establish friendship with Lord Ram which eventually helped Sugreeva get back his lost kingdom and have Bali slayed. O great Monkey Lord! Who does not know your capacity and renown to end distress? ||2||

अंगद के सँग लेन गए सिय खोज, कपीस ये बैन उचारौ
जीवित ना बचि हो हम सों जु, बिना सुधि लाए इहाँ पग धारौ
हेरि थके तट सिन्धु सबै, तब लाइ सिया सुधि प्रान उबारौ
को नहिं जानत है जग में कपि संकट मोचन नाम तिहारौ

अर्थ: सीता की खोज करने के लिए सुग्रीव के द्वारा प्रेरित वानरदल जब अंगद के नेतृत्व में चलने लगा तो सुग्रीव ने चेतावनी दी थी कि यदि सीता का पता लगाए बिना ये लोग वापस लौटे तो वह सबको मार डालेगा। यह वानरदल खोजते-खोजते समुद्र तट तक पहुँच गया पर सीता का पता नहीं लग पाया। सब हारे-थके समुद्र तट पर बैठे थे, तब हे कपि-श्रेष्ठ आपने ही लंका जाकर सीता का पता लगाया था और सबके प्राण बचाए थे। हे हनुमान जी! आपके संकट दूर करने वाले नाम और यश को कौन नहीं जानता।।३।।

Angad ke sang len gaye Siya khoja Kapeesa ye bain uchāro
Jeevit nā bachi ho hum son ju, binā sudhi lāye ihan pag dhāro
Heri thake tat Sindhu sabei, tab lai Siyā-sudhi prān ubāro
Ko nahin jānat hai jag men Kapi sankat-mochan nām tihāro ||3||

When on the advice of Sugreeva a squad of selected monkeys was going in the search of Sita, their ruler, Sugreeva had warned them that should they return without finding whereabouts of Sita, he would have all of them massacred. The squad had reached upto the sea-shore but got no trace of Sita. All were sitting there dawdled and forlorn, when, O Lord, you jumped across the sea and reached Lanka to find Sita. Thus you saved their life by bringing the news about Sita. O great monkey Lord! Who does not know of your capacity and renown to end distress? ||3||

रावन त्रास दई सिय को, तब राक्षसि सौं कहि सोक निवारौ
ताहि समय हनुमान महाप्रभु, जाय महा रचनीचर मारौ
चाहत सीय असोक सौं आगि, सो दै प्रभु मुद्रिका सोकनिवारौ
को नहिं जानत है जग में कपि संकट मोचन नाम तिहारौ।।४।।

अर्थ: लंका में अशोकवाटिका में स्थित सीता जी को जब रावण द्वारा प्रेरित राक्षसियाँ सता रही थीं तो त्रिजटा नामक सहृदय राक्षसी से सीता जी ने शोक निवारण हेतु प्रार्थना की थी। तब त्रिजटा ने राक्षसियों को अपना रावण के नाश का सपना बताकर उन्हें सीता को त्रास देने से रोका था उस समय सीता जी अपने दुख से परेशान होकर अशोक वृक्ष से अग्नि की कामना कर रही थी जिससे वह जलकर मर सकें। तब अशोक वृक्ष पर बैठे हनुमान जी, आपने श्री राम की मुद्रिका (अंगूठी) उनके सामने फेंकी और अपना परिचय देकर उनका शोक निवारण किया और भयंकर राक्षसों, अक्षयकुमार आदि का संहार किया था। हे हनुमान जी, आपके ऐसे संकट दूर करने वाले नाम और यश से इस संसार में कौन परिचित नहीं हैं? कौन नहीं जानता है कि आपका नाम, हे कपि, ही समस्त संकटों को दूर करने में सक्षम है ।।४।।

Rāvan tras dayee Siya ko, tab Rakshasi son kahi sok nrivāro
Tahi samaya Hanumān Mahāprabhu, Jaya Maha-Rajanichar māro
Chahat Siya Ashok son āgi, so dei Prabhu mudrikā sok nivāro
Ko nahin jānat hai jag men, kapi sankat-mochan nām tihāro ||4||

When Sita was being tormented by the demonesses on the advice of Ravan in the Ashoka-grove of Lanka, Sita requested for redemption from a noble hearted demoness named Trijata who then told her companions about a dream she had dreamt in which she saw Ravan destroyed. When all of them retired, Sita requested the Ashoka tree she was sitting beneath to grant her some fire so that she could end her life by burning herself. At that very moment, you, Lord Hanuman, seated on a branch of the tree, threw the ring down before Sita which you had received from Lord Ram as an object of recognition. Then you revealed yourself before Sita and removed her distress by slaying the demon sentinels and Ravan's son Akshya Kumar. O Lord Hanuman, who does not know of your renown and capacity to end distress? ||4||

बान लगौ उर लछमन के, तब प्रान तज्यौ, सुत रावण मारौ
लै गृह वैद्य सुषेन समेत, तबै गिरि द्रोण सुबीर उबारौ
लाइ संजीवनि हाथ दई तब, लक्षमन के तुम प्रान उबारौ
को नहिं जानत है जग में, कपि संकट मोचन नाम तिहारौ ।।५।।

अर्थ: रावण के पुत्र मेघनाद के द्वारा लंका युद्ध में लक्ष्मण के उपर जब शक्तिबाण छोड़ा तो उससे उन्हें प्राणान्तक मूर्च्छा हो गई। तब आप लंका के गृह-वैद्य सुषेण को लाए और उसके द्वारा बताई संजीवनी बूटी लाने के लिए हिमालय पर गए और द्रोण गिरि समेट यह बूटी उखाड़ कर लाए और लक्ष्मण जी की प्राण रक्षा की। इस प्रकार आपने अपने प्रभु की परेशानियाँ दूर कीं। आपके ऐसे संकट दूर करने वाले नाम और यश को संसार में नहीं कौन जानता? ।।५।।

Ban lagau ur Lachman ken, tab prā n tajyo, sut Rāvan māro
Lei griha vaidya Sushen samet, tabe giri drona subeer upāro
Lai sanjeevan hāth dayee tab, Lachaman ke tum prān ubāro
Ko nahin jānat hai jag men, Kapi sankat-mochan nām tihāro ||5||

When the son of Ravan, Meghanad, hurled the shakti-arrow at Lakshman, he was fatally wounded. Then, it was you, O Lord, who brought Lanka's house physician, Sushen, who recommended the life-reviving herb Sanjeevani Booti, to get which you went to the Himalayas and unable to recognise the herb, uprooted the whole of the Drona giri, upon which this herb grew. Thus you brought the medicine in time and saved Laskhman's life. O Lord Hanuman, who does not know your renown and capacity to end distress? ||5||

रावण युद्ध अजान कियो तब, नाग की फॉस सबै सिर डारौ
श्री रघुवी समेत सबै दल, मोह भयौ, यह संकट भारौ
आनि खगेस तबै हनुमान जु, बन्धन काटि सो त्रास निवारौ
को नहिं जानत है जग में, कपि संकट मोचन नाम तिहारौ॥६॥

अर्थ: अज्ञानी रावण ने परब्रह्म के अवतार श्री राम के साथ युद्ध ठान लिया तथा उनको और उनके दल को नाग पाश में जकड़ लिया था। उसकी इस माया से राम-दल मोह में पड़ गया और भारी संकट आन पड़ी। तब हे हनुमान जी! आप ही पक्षिराज गरुड़ को लाए थे जिन्होंने नागपाश को काट कर राम-दल का यह संकट दूर किया था आपके ऐसे संकट मोचन यश और नाम को जगत में कौन नहीं जानता? ॥६॥

Rāvan yuddha ajān kiyo tab, nāg ki phāns sabe sir dāro
Shree Raghuvir samet sabei dal, moh bhayo, yeh sankat bhāro
Aani khages tabei Hanumān ju, bandhan kati su trās nirvāro
Ko nahin jānat hai jag men, Kapi sankat-mochan nām tihāro ||6||

When ignorant Ravan decided to take on the incarnation of Supreme Being, Lord Ram, he fought a magical war and tied all the forces of Lord Ram including the Lord himself in the noose of a serpent. Ravana's this trick distressed whole of Lord Ram's forces. Then you, Lord Hanuman, invoked Garuda, the Lord of the birds, and made him remove the noosc and end the distress. O Lord Hanuman, who does not know your renown and capacity to end distress? ||6||

बन्धु समेत जबै अहिरावण, लै रघुनाथ पाताल सिधारौ
देविहि पूजि भली विधि सों, बलि देउँ सबै मिलि मंत्र उचारौ
जाइ सहाय भयौ तबही, अहिरावण सेन समेत संहारौ
को नहिं जानता है जग में, कपि संकट मोचन नाम तिहारौ।।७।।

अर्थ: जब अहिरावण श्री राम को बन्धु लक्ष्मण सहित चुराकर पाताल ले गया था और उसने सब साथियों से मिलकर यह सलाह की कि अपनी आराध्या देवी की भली-भाँति पूजा कर इन दोनों को बलि देवी पर चढ़ा दी जाय तभी हे कपि! आप सहायक बन कर वहाँ पहुँच गए थे और अहिरावण को सेना सहित संहार कर श्रीराम का यह संकट दूर किया था। आपके ऐसे संकट-मोचन नाम और यश को संसार में कौन नहीं जानता? ।।७।।

Bandhu samet jabai Ahirāvan, lei Raghunāth patal sidhāro
Devahi pooji bhali vidhi son, bali deun sabei mili mantra uchāro
Jai sahaya bhayo tab hee, Ahirāvan sen samet samhāro
Ko nahin jānat hai jag mein, Kapi sankat-mochan nām tihāro ||7||

When Ahiravan kidnapped Lord Ram and Laskhman and went to the nether world, he consulted his companions and decided to sacrifice both the brothers at the altar of his chosen deity. After due ceremony, when he was about to do so, O Lord Hanuman, you reached there in time to slay Ahiravan and his demons and dispelled the death hovering over Lord Ram and Lakshman's life. O Lord Hanuman, who does not know your renown and capacity to end distress? ||7||

काज किए बड़ देवन के, तुम वीर महाप्रभु देखि बिचारौ
कौन-सौ संकटमोर गरीब को, जो तुम से नहिं जात है टारौ
बेगि हरौ हनुमान महाप्रभु, जो कछु संकट होय हमारौ
को नहिं जानत है जग में, कपि संकट मोचन नाम तिहारौ॥८॥

अर्थ: हे महावीर! हे महाप्रभु! आपने देवताओं के बड़े-बड़े कार्य सिद्ध किए हैं। विचारिए तो सही, मुझ गरीब का ऐसा कौन संकट हो सकता है जो तुम से टाला नहीं जा सकता? हे महाप्रभु! मैं तो आपसे यही प्रार्थना करता हूँ कि जो भी मेरा संकट है उसको शीघ्र दूर कीजिए। आपके संकट मोचन नाम और यश को संसार में सभी जानते हैं। यह सर्वविदित है। अब आप मुझ पर भी कृपा कीजिए॥८॥

Kaji kiye bar devan ke, tum veer Mahāprabhu dekhi bichāro
Kaunso sankat mor gareeb ko, jo tum sen nahin jat hai tāro
Begi harau Hanumān Mahāprabhu, jo kachu sankat hoya hamāro
Ko nahin jānat hai jag mein, Kapi sankat-mochan nām tihāro ||8||

O Supremely Valiant! O Great Lord! You have accomplised many big missions for the gods. Just think about poor me; which of my troubles you cannot remove? O Lord, I request you to redeem me and end all the afflictions and distresses that are troubling me. Kindly do it quickly Lord! Who does not know your renown and capacity to end distress. [You have done it for others, Lord now it is my turn. Please end my distress also]. ||8||

एक पद (गीत)
('विनय-पत्रिका' से)

जाकें गति है हनुमान की
ताकि पैज पूजि आई, यह रेखा कुलिस पषान की।
अघटित घटनि सुघट विघटन, अस विरुदावलि नहिं आन की।
सुमिरत संकट सोच विमोचनि मूरत मोद निधान की।।
ता पर सानुकूल गिरिजा हर लखन राम और जानकी।
तुलसी कपि की कृपा विलोकनि खानि सकल कल्यान की।

जिसकी पहुँच श्री हनुमान तक है उसकी कही बात पत्थर पर वज्र द्वारा खींची गई लकीर से भी दृढ़तर और शाश्वत होती है। वह चाहे जो कह दे, वह हो जाता है। जो अघटनीय घटना है वह घटित और घटनीय अघटित हो जाती है- अर्थात् होनी तो अनहोनी करने वाले हनुमान जी हैं और ऐसी यश गथा किसी अन्य की नहीं। जिनके स्मरण मात्र से सारे संकटों के बादल छँट जाते हैं ऐसी आनन्द स्वरूप मूर्ति किस और की है-सिवा हनुमान जी के। हनुमान जी स्वयं ही इतने सक्षम और सुख-निधान हैं, उस पर पार्वती, शंकरजी, श्री राम लक्ष्मण ओर जानकी उन पर विशेषरूप से कृपालु है। (स्वाभाविक है) कि उनकी कृपा अगर किसी पर हो जाए तो उसको समझना चाहिए मानों उसे हर प्रकार के कल्याण की खान मिल गई है- अर्थात् उसका हर प्रकार कल्याण ही कल्याण है।

(xiii) A Song
(From 'Vinaya Patrika')

Jāken gati hai Hanumān ki
Tāki paija pooji āyee, yeh rekhā kulish pashān ki |
Aghatit ghatani sughat vighatan, as virudāvali nahin ān ki |
Sumirat sankat socha vimochan moortati mod nidhān ki |
Ta par sanukoola Girija, Har, Lakhan, Ram aur Jānaki |
Tulsi Kapi ki kripa vilokani khāni sakal kalyān ki |

He who has access to Lord Hanuman has his pledge always fulfilled and his utterance becomes more true and firm than the line cast on stone by the thunderbolt. His predictions always come true. Even the most impossible happening takes place quite naturally and the most commonplace occurrence becomes very rare. That is, such a person develops the capacity to alter even the course of time because, the controller of time, Lord Hanuman is his protector. For no other god is renowned for rendering so much help to his devotee. Who else has more auspicious, bliss-giving visage than Lord Hanuman, the very remembrance of whom is enough to scatter away all the clouds of sorrow and remove all distress. Lord Hanuman is himself so competent and powerful and on the top of it he is the darling of Goddess Parvati, Lord Shankar, Lord Ram, Lakshman and mother Janaki. Hence it is obvious that he on whom Lord Hanuman sheds his grace should consider himself singularly lucky because this grace ensures all kinds of happiness and prosperity. Such a fortunate person has his welfare assured in every way.

तुलसीदास कृत एक प्रसिद्ध लोक भजन

निम्नलिखित भजन तुलसीदास के जीवन की एक प्रमुख घटना का लोक भाषा वर्णन करता है। जब तुलसी अपनी पत्नी रत्नावली के प्रेम में पागल होकर भयंकर वर्षा और अन्य प्राकृतिक उत्पातों को पार कहते हुए रत्नावली के पास (उसके मायके में) पहुँचे तो उनकी पत्नी ने उन्हें फटकारा था। तभी से तुलसीदास के मन में राम भक्ति का उदय हुआ और वे गोस्वामी बन गए।

काहे न तुलसी राम कहौ रे!
काहे न तुलसी राम कहौ रे!
गहरी-नदिया अगम बहति ही, मुर्दा जाति बहौ रे!
तुलसी जानी नाव बहति है, ताहि पै चढ़ि तुलसी पार गयौ रे!
महलन-महलन हम फिरि आए दरवज्जौ न मिलौ रे।
खिड़की में इक अजगर लटक्यौ, ताहि पकड़ तुलसी महल चढ़ौ रे!
ऐसी प्रीति मोरे हाड़ चाम सौ, हरि सों क्यों न करौ रे!
लाइ बसौ बैकुन्ठ लोक में, देवन को दरबार लगौ रे।
तू तिरिया मोरे धरम की माता, तें मोहि ग्यान दयौ रे!
तुलसीदास भजौं भगवाना, आजु सों तिरिया तेरी सेज न चढ़ौ रे!
काहे न तुलसी राम कहौ रे!

(xiv) A Famous Folk-bhajan by Tulsidas

[The following devotional song depicts the most important event of Tulsidas's life in a very engrossing manner. He had gone to meet his wife in her native place despite all troubles. But he was admonished for his infatuation for the sensual body. Since then Tulsidas developed love for Ram.]

Kāhe na Tulsi, Rām kaho re!
Kāhe na Tulsi, Rām kaho re!
Gaharee nadiya agam bahat hee, murda jati baho re
Tulsi jani nava bahat hai, tahee pe chadi Tulsi pār baho re!
Mahalan-mahalan ham phir aye, darwajjo na milo re
Khidakhee men ik ajāgar latkyo, tahi pakad Tulsi mahal chado re!
Eisee preeti more haad-chaam so, Hari son kyo na karo re
Jai basyo Vaikuntha lok me, devan ko darbar lago re!
Tu tiriya more dharam kee mātā, ten mohi gyān dayo re!
Tulsidas bhajon bhagwana, aj son tiriya teri sej na chadyo re!
Kahe na tulsi, Ram kaho re!

अर्थः हे तुलसी! तू राम का नाम क्यों नहीं लेता है। तब तुलसी अपनी विवशता बताते हैं। रत्नावली के मायके जाने पर प्रेम में पागल होकर तुलसी रात को ही घर से बाहर आए। तब गहरी नदी (जमुना) उफन कर बह रही थी। कोई नाव वाला उन्हें पार ले जाने को राजी नहीं हुआ तो भी वह नदी में कूद पड़े और एक मुर्दे को नाव समझ कर उसी के सहारे से नदी पार की।

जब रत्नावली के घर पहुँचे तो घर के सब दरवाजे उस अंधियारी भयंकर दृष्टि पूर्ण रात में बन्द थे। जब कहीं से उन्हें प्रवेश नहीं मिला तो खिड़की पर लटके एक अजगर के सहारे अन्दर पहुँचे । रत्नावली ने जब उनका यह पागलपन देखा तो उन्हें बहुत फटकारा। उन्होंने कहा ऐसी प्रीति तुमने मेरे हाड़-चाम नश्वर-शरीर से क्यों लगा रखी है। हे नाथ! अच्छा होता कि आप ऐसी प्रीति (हरि) से करते तो बैकुन्ठ में आपका निवास होता और देवताओं के दरबार में आपका सम्मान होता। यह सुनकर तुलसीदास को बोध हुआ और उन्होंने कहाः हे स्त्री! तू वाकई में मेरी धर्म-माता है क्योंकि तूने मुझे ज्ञान दिया है। अब से मैं प्रण करता हूँ कि भगवान का भजन ही करूँगा और तेरी सेज न चढ़ूँगा, अर्थात् सब माया मोह के बन्धन त्याग दूँगा।

O Tulsi, Why don't you chant the name of Ram. A deep river was flowing in spate. Tulsi mistook a floating dead body to be a boat, used it to go across the river.

(Reaching Ratna's home) When I couldn't find an entry into the house I broke into the house by climbing up with the help of a hanging python. (Reaching inside, he was scolded by his wife). So much love you have for my fey-body made of bones and skin. If you could have even a little of this for Lord Ram, you would have earned praises from even the gods.

(Stung to the quick, Tulsidas says) : "Hey woman! You are my god-mother since you have enlightened me with knowledge. Henceforth I shall only chant god's name and shall never come to your bed."

